NatWest Business Handbooks

Financial Control

David Irwin

Pitman Publishing
128 Long Acre, London WC2E 9AN
A Division of Longman Group UK Limited

First published in Great Britain in association with the National Westminster Bank,
1991

© Longman Group UK Ltd 1991

British Library Cataloguing in Publication Data
Irwin, David
    Financial control. − (NatWest business handbooks)
    I. Title II. Series
    338.6

ISBN 0 273 03391 3

Typeset, printed and bound in Great Britain

Contents

To Jane and Catherine
for their love and encouragement

Preface

This book is intended to help the owner/managers of small businesses, employing up to 25 people, and who still have control of all the key decisions and are responsible for all the administration. It should also be helpful to all those who are responsible for financial planning and financial control in a small business. Its aim is to show the importance of good financial control and to suggest ways in which that can be done.

The book follows a logical progression from demonstrating the need for good control and understanding financial statements through budgeting and preparing financial plans to collecting the figures and using them to exercise control. Whilst most benefit will be derived from reading the entire book, the reader can read those chapters regarded as immediately necessary; and whilst a knowledge of basic book-keeping will be helpful, a review of appropriate book-keeping techniques is included. The reader requiring a greater understanding of book-keeping should refer to *Book-keeping and Accounting* in the NatWest Business Handbooks series.

By the end of the book, the reader should:

- Understand how good financial control helps in the management of a business.
- Be able to formulate a financial strategy.
- Understand how financial and management control can be achieved through simple documentation.
- Understand the appropriate techniques to solve problems identified through the financial control procedures.
- Be aware of the ways in which computers can be used to help you keep control.

I would particularly like to thank Peter Westgarth, Dan Brophy, Gordon Kinghorn, Hew Irwin and Bill Hudspeth for reading early drafts and for their helpful comments.

Acknowledgements

I am extremely grateful to the following who have provided examples
to illustrate the text:

Centre for Interfirm Comparison;
ICC Business Publications Ltd;
National Westminster Bank plc;
Young & Co's Brewery plc; and
the many clients who have inspired other examples.

David Irwin
Newcastle-upon-Tyne, January 1991

1   Is your business profitable?

Introduction □ Why are you in business? □ The importance of making a profit □ What are the key activities for success? □ Planning and monitoring □ Some basic terms □ Conclusion and checklist

Introduction

All businesses experience problems. Some of these problems are beyond your control, such as interest rates or the latest consumer fad. Many problems, however, need not arise if a little care is taken to ensure that you understand what is happening at all times. Look at how many businesses, apparently successful, have gone bankrupt through over-trading. Wildly exceeding your sales forecast can cause cashflow problems as severe as failing to reach the forecast. By the end of this chapter, you should understand which are the most important aspects of your business over which to exercise control and, in particular, appreciate the importance of good financial control.

Why are you in business?

Surveys of people thinking of starting in business suggest that most people wish to start their own business to make money. Surveys of people who have already started in business suggest that most people continue in business because they value the independence of being their own boss. Of course, this may reflect the reality that it is difficult to make a fortune from running your own business. Many people who do run their own business are able to manage very comfortably without necessarily wanting the extra stress of considerable growth. Whether you want a business which is aiming for rapid growth, or just to support you and your family, it is important to make a profit from running the business. That has to be the first and foremost objective.

You should also enjoy what you do. One of the great benefits of working for oneself is the opportunity to do work that is fun and rewarding. Of course, there will be tasks, as with any job, that may seem tedious and time-consuming, but overall you should be seeking a balance of fun and reward.

The importance of making a profit

Without a profit you cannot reward the investors for their stake in the business (including yourself if you are the sole investor), nor will you have enough money for reinvestment to make the business grow. To do that you need a product or service which is marketable and which you can persuade customers to buy.

Large companies generally aim to maximise their profits over the long term. This increases shareholder value and gives the investors a regular dividend. Private companies do not need to worry about profit maximisation if they choose not to. They are not vulnerable to takeovers and the shareholders may have other objectives. Working shareholders, sole proprietors or partners may agree, for example, to forego some of the potential profit because they prefer to work less hard. However, if you do not aim for a realistic profit, there is always the danger that you will make a loss and businesses which lose money quickly cease to trade.

If you have invested money in the business, is the reward greater than the opportunity cost? If, for example, you have £20 000 available you might receive interest of 10 per cent (after tax) from the bank or building society. If you use that money for your business instead, then you need to aim to generate a return better than 10 per cent, as well as the business paying your salary. Otherwise, there is an opportunity cost equal to the difference in the return. In that case you might decide that you would be better off working for someone else and reinvesting your money elsewhere.

Similarly, if you need to borrow money from the bank, you need to ensure that you are generating a return that is considerably greater than the interest that you have to pay the bank, otherwise you end up working for the bank manager instead of yourself.

Many people do not think carefully enough about the cost of borrowing money, only looking at the monthly repayments. But it is an important consideration. Later, we will look at ways of assessing whether the cost of money is too high relative to the profit of the business.

Naturally, there will be occasions when you need to borrow large sums of money, perhaps for short periods. This will be far easier if your business is profitable and if you can demonstrate to potential lenders, such as the banks, that you are in control and know the exact financial position of the business.

What are the key activities for success?

There are four major aspects of running a business which need particular care if the business is to be successful.

First, the business has to be able to provide a product or service efficiently, of the right quality and at an acceptable cost.

Second, the product or service must be effectively promoted to the prospective customer. The customer must be prepared to pay more for the benefits that they derive than it costs you to provide the features. The difference between cost and price is your profit. We will be looking at the relationship between cost and price in some detail later. Exhibit 1.1 shows the differences between features and benefits.

Feature	Benefit
Leather seats	Comfort
Anti-lock brakes	Safety
Central locking	Security
1400cc lean burn engine	Economy
Hatchback	Convenience

Exhibit 1.1 Features and benefits for a motor car

Third, you need to exercise tight financial control. It is extremely easy for the costs to run away, to waste materials and to sell your product or service too cheaply. At best, this will reduce your profit; at worst, you will make a loss and, eventually, cease to trade.

Finally, you need to be aware of the business's human resource needs. Once you start to employ people you will have to think about recruitment, induction, career development, training, motivation, etc. This all costs extra money, but you should regard it as an investment in exactly the same way as you might expect to invest in machinery. The business depends on the people employed, so treat them properly.

Running a business means that you are continually faced with a series of events for which decisions have to be taken. The right decisions depend upon having the right information easily available. This is as true for information about the business's financial position as for every other aspect of running the business.

Planning and monitoring

You should regard financial control as part of an integrated management system for your business, which includes setting strategic objectives, planning and forecasting, budgeting, recording data, comparing performance against the plan and exercising control. Some variance is to be expected, but if the performance varies from the plan too much then corrective action will be required. If it is not possible to correct the cause of the variation, then some re-

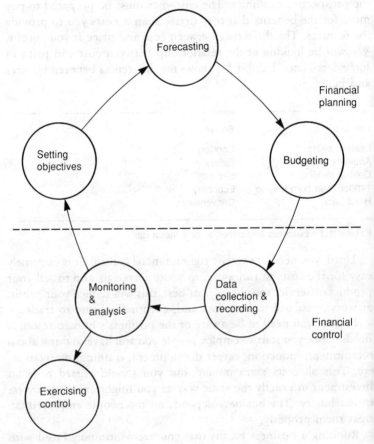

Exhibit 1.2 Management cycle

planning will be required. Part 3 of the book looks at the planning process in some detail.

It is usually relatively straightforward to take decisions about capital expenditure. You can assess the need for a piece of equipment or a new vehicle; you can see what it will cost and know whether you have or can borrow the money. It becomes more difficult if you need more than one item but cannot afford everything, although there are techniques to help you choose.

It is considerably more difficult, however, to control working capital. This is the money effectively tied up in stock, owed to you by customers, etc.

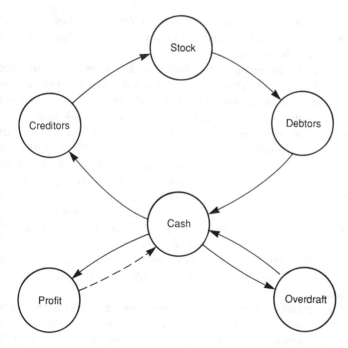

Exhibit 1.3 Working capital cycle

You will require to finance stock, which includes raw materials, work in progress and finished goods. (Even if you are a service-based business you may well hold raw materials or have what is effectively work in progress.) Once you deliver those goods (or services) to your customer then you have sold them. But you may not be paid for some time. The eventual payment releases cash which can be used to pay your suppliers, to pay the fixed costs (including your time), and may also provide a profit.

If you have to pay your creditors faster than your debtors pay you then you will need to borrow money from the bank, normally as an overdraft. Retained profit is also often used to cover at least some of this working capital requirement.

You will need to think carefully about all these needs and incorporate them, together with your sales forecast, into a budget. If you get your budgeting right, then you should have a fair idea of what your income and expenditure is likely to be during the year.

Some basic terms

Most terms will be described the first time that they are used. However, some will be used frequently throughout the book so it seems sensible to describe them here.

Revenue is the income of a business. It relates to a particular accounting period. Deducting all the expenses for that period determines the *profit*. *Gross profit* is normally regarded as the revenue less the 'cost of sales'; i.e., the costs directly attributable to the sales. For example, a business buys wood, turns the wood into furniture and sells the furniture. The cost of the wood is the cost of sales. *Net profit* is the gross profit less all the other expenses. If you are self-employed as a sole trader or partner in a partnership, the profit is yours. You are not paid a wage but take a share of the profit. Any profit remaining can be reinvested in the business or used as working capital. If you own a company, then you are an employee and are paid a wage. If successful, there will still be a profit to provide working capital or for reinvestment to pay dividends to the shareholders. Definitions of different types of cost will be looked at later.

The *liquidity* of a business is a measure of its working capital or cash position. Generally, the cash available will be shown on the cashflow forecast. A business can still be profitable and run out of funds, by having too much stock or by allowing customers credit periods which are too generous.

A business starts with £1 000, buys one widget and sells it for £1 500 cash. The business now has £1 500. It buys a further widget for £1 000 and sells it for £1 500 but this customer does not pay for a month. The business cannot buy any more stock until either the customer pays or the owner introduces another £500 to buy more stock.

Exhibit 1.4   Liquidity

Sometimes businesses discover that there is considerable demand for their product. They buy more stock, make more goods, sell more products – all apparently at a profit. But then they discover that their customers do not pay soon enough whilst their suppliers are demanding payment. This is known as *over-trading*.

A business is *solvent* if it has sufficient assets (cash, stock, debtors, etc) to cover its liabilities (loans, creditors, etc). If it doesn't have this cover then it is *trading whilst insolvent*, which is now an offence. Thus, a business must be able to meet its debts as they become due. If you cannot turn your assets into cash to pay those debts, then you might still become insolvent even though your assets apparently exceed your liabilities. Sole traders and partnerships have always had *unlimited liability*: that means that they are liable for all debts incurred by the business. Companies normally have *limited liability*: the shareholders will lose only their investment if the business fails. However, if it can be demonstrated that the directors knew a company was trading whilst insolvent, then they can be held to be personally liable.

The need for control: conclusion and checklist

By now you probably recognise the major reasons for keeping tight financial control. These include:
● Monitoring performance against plan.
● Maximising profitability.
● Assessing solvency.
● Watching liquidity.

If you are able to do all of these effectively and efficiently then you will have the basis of sound financial control. You should be able to avoid cashflow problems – instead you will be in a position to visit your bank manager, explain your circumstances and negotiate further loan facilities.

Evidence of poor control is demonstrated by:

● A lack of clear objectives for the business;
● A lack of knowledge of the basic information necessary to run a business successfully;
● A lack of appreciation of the cash needs of the business for a given rate of activity; and
● A tendency to assume that poor results stem from economic conditions or even bad luck.

8 The need for financial control

Are you aware of your current position? Can you, right now, answer all of the following questions.

- How much money have you tied up in working capital? £ _____

- What is your current bank balance? £ _____

- How long do your customers take before they pay? _____ days

- Are you solvent? _____

- What is the return on your capital? _____ %

- What is your net profit on sales? _____ %

If you can answer all of those questions then you probably don't need this book. Otherwise, read on.

2 Collecting the information

Introduction

In the first chapter, the importance of planning and then monitoring performance against the plan was emphasised. This is only possible if the right data is collected and recorded. This chapter explains the importance of keeping appropriate financial records in a simple and straightforward manner and will help you to assess whether you are collecting the right information.

Why keep records?

Have you ever sat down quietly and thought about the information that would help you control your business more effectively – or is your record-keeping driven by external requirements, such as the Inland Revenue, the VAT inspectors, or the fact that company law insists that you keep accounts?

Record-keeping has to serve three purposes:

1. To provide information which can be used to help in the preparation of next year's plan;
2. To provide appropriate information for day to day management control of the business; and
3. To provide all the information for the preparation of annual accounts and statutory returns.

The second of these is the most important for monitoring and control of the business. Unfortunately, too many owner/managers believe that they can wait until the end of the year, after which their accountant will tell them how well they are doing. This is a mistake because:

- Published accounts are intended for public consumption (e.g. Inland Revenue, government, shareholders, etc) and often hide as much as they reveal;
- The annual accounts are historical, often not available until some months after the year to which they relate; and
- The annual accounts do not provide the relevant information for management decisions.

A business must record every financial transaction. How it does this will depend on the size and nature of the business. A business run entirely on cash will need only a cash book plus the supporting invoices. However, very few businesses are entirely run on cash in this age of credit. Like cash, credit needs to be carefully controlled to ensure the health of the business.

If all these records are kept well and are easy to read, not only will they provide the information that you need, but they will also make it easier for you or your accountant to prepare your end of year accounts. The end of year accounts are fine for the shareholders and the Inland Revenue, but they are produced far too late to exercise tight control. For that, you require management accounts, produced regularly and giving the essential information to help you and your staff ensure that you are on target.

Accounting records are not only the books used to record the business transactions but also include all the invoices both issued and received by the business. The business should file its records in an orderly manner, including purchase invoices, copy sales invoices, etc, as this will assist in keeping accurate accounting records.

The accounting records need to be detailed enough to enable you to be able to say at any time what the position of the business is: i.e. How much cash have you in the business? How much do you owe? How much are you owed? How big is your overdraft?

What records should I keep?

All your financial information is derived from your book-keeping system. Whilst some of the techniques may appear more appropriate for larger businesses, they will all help very small businesses as well.

A reliable, easy to use accounting system is, therefore, essential if your monitoring is going to be straightforward and if your control is to be effective. It is easy to underestimate the problems encountered in collecting relevant data, so take the time and thought to set up an effective and efficient system.

There are many computerised book-keeping systems available but it probably makes sense to set up a manual system which you completely understand. This can then be speeded up by computerising at a later date – the danger of not understanding the system is that errors, which inevitably creep in, will not be spotted.

Whether you use a proprietary book-keeping system or set up your own using cash analysis books, you need a system which will enable you to collect all the relevant data and convert that data to provide you with up-to-date management accounts.

The data to record includes:

2

- Orders placed with the business.
- Sales.
- Invoices issued by the business for sales.
- Invoices received by the business for purchases.
- Cash receipts.
- Cash expenditure.

This data will enable you to prepare:

- Production schedules; and
- Purchasing requirements;

and to monitor:

- Liquidity and solvency;
- Stock levels of raw materials, work in progress and finished goods;
- Aged debtors; and
- Aged creditors.

All cash transactions should be recorded immediately. But it will help monitoring considerably if you maintain a sales ledger and purchase ledger so that assets and liabilities can be quickly calculated. These requirements are looked at in more detail in Chapter 9.

You need to have the information as quickly as possible. It is better to have 80 per cent of the data immediately than 100 per cent when it is too late to use. Try not to generate too much or you will find it difficult to use. One business, for example, simply generates a list of aged debtors every week and keeps chasing them to pay.

Do not collect information that is unlikely to be useful.

Turning the data into graphs, tables, charts, etc can help by revealing trends, which in turn helps in the revision of forecasts and future planning. Some computer spreadsheets have extremely good graphics and are very effective in this role.

Statutory requirements

Each year the Inland Revenue will want to know how much profit your business made in its previous year in order to assess you for the tax due. If you do not supply accounts showing how much your business made then the Inland Revenue will estimate the profit they think the business has made and assess you accordingly. This could lead to a demand for more tax than you should be paying.

It is important not to under-disclose sales of the business, for example, by netting off payments, as the Inland Revenue will charge penalties and interest on any tax not paid at the correct time. They have techniques based on the analysis of similar types of business which enable them to check whether it is likely that sales have been made for cash and not included in the figures in the accounts.

If you employ staff, you must deduct their income tax and national insurance under the pay as you earn (PAYE) scheme and send it to the Inland Revenue each month. They also insist on the way that records relating to wages and tax are kept.

If you are registered for VAT, as most businesses are, then the VAT regulations require you to keep accounts and that the VAT element is shown separately in those accounts. A quarterly return must then be provided to the VAT inspectors. There are considerable penalties for late payment but preparing the VAT return is simple and straightforward provided all the figures are recorded in your book-keeping system.

If your business is incorporated (i.e. it is a company), then you must have your accounts audited every year by a chartered accountant. These must then be filed at Companies House. Small businesses can, however, file a modified form of account instead of the full accounts, though they still have to prepare full accounts for the Inland Revenue. Once accounts are filed, they are in the public domain. You would probably choose, therefore, to file modified accounts in order not to give away too much about your business.

Collecting information: conclusion and checklist

Collecting the right information is a vital prerequisite for monitoring and controlling any business's finances. Every accountant seems to have the client whose accounting system is two shoe boxes – one for invoices issued and one for bills received – which the accountant is then given at the end of the year and expected to turn into sensible accounts. You will have an effective book-keeping system if:

● You record every transaction immediately (or at least by the end of the day);
● You maintain a sales ledger and a purchase ledger in addition to the main cash book; and
● You are able to derive key information quickly and easily.

---

3   Final accounts

3

Introduction

Do you look at published accounts and wonder what they all mean? The financial statements paint a picture of how well, or otherwise, a business has done. By the end of this chapter, you should understand how the basic financial statements are calculated and what they mean.

What are the basic financial statements?

There are three basic financial statements: the balance sheet; the profit and loss account; and the cashflow statement.

The *balance sheet* summarises the state of a business at a specific point in time. The *profit and loss account* shows how a business performed over a specific period, between two balance sheets, and records the total revenue and expenditure for that period.

The *cashflow statement* (also known as flow of funds statement or statement of sources and uses of funds) shows how cash flowed to, from and within the business. A forecast of cashflow is one of the most important management accounting tools. It is an estimate of the cash needs of the business for the next trading period. Cashflow forecasts are reviewed in more detail in Chapter 7.

Accounting simply follows the money flowing within, to and from a business. The accounts reflect the financial position of the business rather than that of the owner.

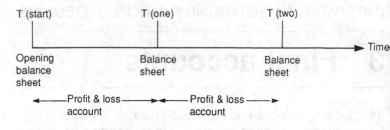

Exhibit 3.1 Financial statements

Understanding balance sheets

The starting point for every business is zero. Every transaction is recorded. All the finance of the business is matched by assets. Another way of stating this is to say that what a business owns (its assets) is always equal to what it owes (its liabilities).

Imagine that you put £1 000 into a business. That is the finance of the business, but it is also a liability – it is money owed to you. If the business leaves the money in the bank, then it has current assets of £1 000. If it buys equipment, it still has assets, now known as fixed assets, of £1 000.

The balance sheet is a financial snapshot and summarises the position of assets and liabilities at a specific point in time. In published accounts this is at the end of your financial year, though a balance sheet can be prepared at any time. It incorporates how much the business owes to suppliers and how much is due from customers. It reflects assets such as equipment and vehicles used in the business and the amount of capital you have invested in the business.

The balance sheet tells you:

- How much capital is employed in the business?
  (How much is the business worth?)
- How liquid is the business?
  (How quickly can the assets be turned into cash?)
- How solvent is the business?
  (What is the likelihood that the business might go bankrupt?)
- How is the business financed?
  (Where does the finance come from and how much of it is loan finance?)

In double entry book-keeping, every financial transaction requires two entries, normally with each entry in a different ledger. The balance sheet is simply a summary of the balances from all the ledgers. Many people no longer use double entry book-keeping but the balance sheet is still essential in understanding the overall picture of the business.

Traditionally, the balance sheet shows the 'finance' or 'liabilities' of the business on the left and the 'assets' of the business on the right.

Source of funds	Application of funds
Finance (liabilities)	Assets

Exhibit 3.2 Balance sheet

Remember, earlier it was stated that the balance sheet reflects the position of the business. Thus money owed to suppliers, or invested by (i.e. owed to) the owners is a source of funds.

The money invested by the owners is usually known as the *capital* if the business is a sole trader or partnership, or *share capital* if it is a company. Combined with earnings retained in the business, it is known as the *equity* or *shareholders' funds* of the business. Those funds are applied to the acquisition of equipment or used for working capital.

Liabilities		Assets	
Equity	1 000	Fixed assets	10 000
Loans	9 500		
	10 500		
Current liabilities	500	Current assets	1 000
	11 000		11 000

Exhibit 3.3 Balance sheet

The *net asset value* is the total assets (£11 000, in the example shown in Exhibit 3.3) less the current liabilities (£500), i.e. £10 500. It is also equal to the equity plus the long-term debt. In general, short-term debts or loans repayable within a year are regarded as current liabilities; loans and other debts falling due after one year are regarded as long-term debt and are usually shown separately on the balance sheet so as not to affect the net current assets. We will return to this in the next chapter when we look at the effect on the control ratios.

The *net worth* of the business equals the total assets (£11 000) less the current liabilities (£500) less the long-term debt (£9 500), i.e. £1 000. This is equal to the shareholders' capital plus the reserves.

Purists will argue that this is the only way to set out a balance sheet. It seems odd to people who are not accountants to add the shareholders' capital and the reserves to the current liabilities. Some people move the current liabilities to the right hand side of the balance sheet and deduct them from the current assets to give a figure known as the net current assets. This is shown in Exhibit 3.4.

Finance			Assets		
Equity		1 000	Fixed assets		10 000
Loans		9 500			
			Current assets	1 000	
			Current liabilities	500	
			Net current assets		500
Net finance		10 500	Net assets		10 500

Exhibit 3.4 Balance sheet: alternative horizontal layout

Some people go further, however, and show the balance sheet as a single column. This is becoming increasingly popular and gives all the required information quickly and easily.

As can be seen, the different layouts of the balance sheet all present exactly the same information, though in a different format.

Fixed assets		
Tangible assets		
Equipment	10 000	
Buildings		
Intangible assets		
Goodwill		
		10 000
Current assets		
Stock		
Debtors		
Cash at bank	1 000	
		1 000
Current liabilities		
Overdraft		
Loans		
Creditors	500	
Tax		500
Net current assets		500
Total assets less current liabilities		10 500
Creditors: falling due after one year		9 500
Capital & reserves		
Capital	1 000	
Reserves		1 000
Long-term liabilities & capital		10 500

Exhibit 3.5   Balance sheet: columnar format

Exhibit 3.5 presents the same information in columnar format. Note that it adds long-term funds to the capital and reserves, giving a net finance figure of £10 500 as in Exhibit 3.4. Some people prefer to deduct long-term creditors from the figure of 'total assets less current liabilities' (see Exhibit 3.6). This is the equivalent of the capital and reserves.

Fixed assets		
Tangible assets		
Equipment	10 000	
Buildings		
Intangible assets		
Goodwill		
		10 000
Current assets		
Stock		
Debtors		
Cash at bank	1 000	
		1 000
Current liabilities		
Overdraft		
Loans		
Creditors	500	
Tax		500
Net current assets		500
Total assets less current liabilities		10 500
Creditors: falling due after one year		9 500
Net assets		1 000
Capital & reserves		
Capital	1 000	
Reserves		
Net finance		1 000

Exhibit 3.6   Balance sheet: columnar format

The net worth of the business can be seen immediately from the balance sheet using this layout. Using this format it is easy to deduct current liabilities from current assets to give net current assets, also known as net working capital. This layout will be retained for later examples.

If the business ceased to trade and you were able to dispose of all the assets at book value, then the amount of money you have left would be equal to the net worth of the business. If you wanted to sell the business as a going concern, the net worth represents its value, although you might get more for *goodwill*.

Goodwill is a representation of the future earning power of a business based on the likelihood that customers have built up a habit of buying from your business and will continue to do so after the business is sold. When a business is purchased, any amount paid in excess of its net worth represents the value placed on goodwill.

Goodwill is often included on the balance sheet as an 'intangible' asset. So is money invested in research and development. The difficulty with this approach is that there is no guarantee that the money will be recovered. It is regarded as good practice, therefore, to write off these intangible assets in the same way that fixed assets are depreciated.

You buy a newsagency with a net worth of £30 000 and an annual profit of £50 000. You agree to pay £75 000. This represents purchase of the assets of £30 000 and goodwill of £45 000.

Exhibit 3.7 Goodwill

You may have read about *price/earnings (p/e) ratios* for publicly quoted companies. This is a similar concept. Investors are prepared to pay a price for shares that is a multiple of the net earnings, i.e. the profit, of the company. In the UK, depending on the sector, the p/e ratio is typically around 12. These are recorded in the financial press. They are a measure of investors' confidence in the future earning capacity of the business. There is no difference, in principle, for a small privately-owned business, though the ratio is likely to be considerably lower.

You will notice one item on balance sheets headed depreciation. If you have fixed assets, equipment for example, it is unlikely that they will be worth as much in three years' time as they are now.

Imagine that you run a machine tool business. You will have invested in a range of machine tools – say, a lathe, a milling machine, a drill, a guillotine, etc – at substantial cost, £30 000 perhaps. These machines are clearly a fixed asset. You have spent £30 000 and have machines worth £30 000. But as soon as you start to use them, they begin to wear out.

It is normal, therefore, to predict the expected life of equipment and 'write off' or 'depreciate' the value over that number of years. If you expect the machine tools to last four years, then you would charge £7 500 depreciation each year. The fixed assets on the balance sheet are reduced by the accumulated depreciation, giving a value known as 'book value', i.e. the value of the equipment as shown in the books.

Understanding profit and loss accounts

The profit and loss account gives an indication of what happened during a specific period, usually a year, and reflects the profit that has been made. The sales figure should be obtained from the sales ledger, being the net sales for the period. It does not reflect the actual cash received from customers since some payments may still be outstanding. Do not confuse the terms 'income and expenditure' with 'receipts and payments'. Income (or revenue) and expenditure relate to the period of the profit and loss. The terms receipts and payments are used to reflect flows of cash during the period.

The profit and loss account tells you how much profit (or loss) was made during the period and usually shows whether this was distributed to the shareholders as dividends, or taken as drawings for a sole trader or partnership, or retained in the business. The part of the profit and loss account which shows this distribution is called the appropriation account.

As explained in Chapter 1, the direct costs of sales are normally deducted from the sales figure to give gross profit. This allows you to calculate your gross profit margin, and compare your business with others which are similar. The overheads are then deducted from the gross profit to give the net profit.

Source of funds	Application of funds
Revenues	Expenses

Exhibit 3.8 Profit and loss statement

A basic principle in accounting is to match costs against the revenues generated by these costs. This includes debtors, creditors, stock and depreciation.

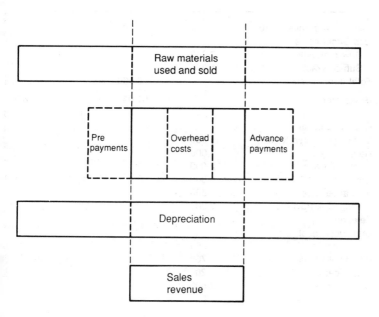

Exhibit 3.9 Matching revenues and costs

To calculate the profit for a period you must determine the costs of the resources used up to generate the revenues for that period. Stock consumed must be charged even if it is not yet paid for. Stock bought but not yet consumed is not charged against that period. Anything paid for in advance of the period, or after the period but consumed during the period, should be included. Anything paid for during the period, but actually attributable to a different period should be excluded. If a machine is used for several years only the depreciation for that period should be charged.

Expenses which relate to the period but not paid until the following period are known as 'accruals' or accrued expenses. These will be included on the balance sheet as current liabilities. Payments made in advance will be shown on the balance sheet as a 'prepayment' under current assets. Some payments may cover two periods so will be split accordingly – this is an example of the matching principle.

Profit which is retained in the business is included on the balance sheet as reserves, i.e. it is a source of funds. Do not confuse reserves with cash available. Like all other sources of funds it might be applied as working capital or tied up in equipment.

Let us now look at an example of a profit and loss account.

Sales: 1 400 units @ 50		70 000
less Direct costs		
Raw materials	7 000	
Sub-contract	1 960	
Total direct costs		8 960
Gross profit		61 040	87%
Overhead costs		
Employee wages & NI	15 000	
Rent & rates	7 000	
Heat, light & power	2 000	
Advertising etc.	5 000	
Insurance	500	
Transport & travel	2 000	
Telephone	1 400	
Stationery, post, etc.	700	
Bank charges	200	
Interest on loan	1 700	
Legal fees	200	
Depreciation	2 500	
Total overheads		38 200
Net profit		22 840	33%
Less: Drawings		15 000
Tax		4 700
Retained in business		3 140

Exhibit 3.10 Profit and loss account

The total sales for the period are £70 000. The direct costs of raw materials and sub-contract costs are those attributable to these sales. All the other costs are deducted to give the net profit. It is usual to show how that profit is divided or appropriated. It can go in three ways: to the shareholders or owners (as drawings or dividends); to the government as tax; or it can be retained in the business. Sometimes interest payments are excluded from the overhead costs and included at the bottom as a distribution of profit. This is because the rate of interest is outside the owner's control and including it as a trading cost can distort the figures. We will look at this again when we look at ratio analysis.

Remember that the profit for the period is not the same as the amount of cash the business has at the end of the period. The main differences are as follows:

1. *Sales income v. cash received.* A sale is recorded at the time that the goods are dispatched or a service provided, irrespective of whether the customer has paid or not. In VAT terms, this is the tax point. If a sale has been effected, but no cash has yet been received, the monies owing will be shown on the balance sheet as a debtor. All the sales during the period are summarised as income in the profit and loss account.

2. *Costs are not the same as cash payments.* Costs are often shown in the profit and loss account as direct costs or overhead costs. Direct costs (sometimes known as cost of sales) reflect the amount of raw materials used in producing the goods that have been sold and any sub-contract costs. A builder, for example, might sub-contract the glazing work – this then becomes a direct cost. If you feel able to hire and fire depending on the amount of work available, some of your labour might also be a direct cost. (Note that this is a simplification – the different sorts of costs are explained in more detail in Chapter 6.)

3

It is the use of raw material stocks, however, which confuses since it is unlikely that all the stock bought in a period will also be consumed in that period.

Nicki starts the year with £2 000 worth of stock, buys £10 000 worth during the year, and has £1 000 worth left at the end of the year.

Opening stock	2 000
add: Purchases	10 000
Total available	12 000
less: Closing stock	1 000
Total consumed	11 000

Exhibit 3.11   Nicki's Nighties

As can be seen in Exhibit 3.11, Nicki's direct costs are £11 000, even though she only spent £10 000 on raw materials during the year. This would still be true even if Nicki had not paid her last bill. This would, however, be shown on the balance sheet as money owing to a creditor.

If some of Nicki's nighties are completed but remain unsold, then there is a further complication. Look at Exhibit 3.12. Note that the finished goods have been valued at the raw material cost.

		Stock	
		Raw materials	Finished goods
Opening stock		2 000	2 000
add: Purchases		10 000	
Total available		12 000	
less: Closing stock		1 000	
Total consumed		11 000	11 000
Total finished goods			13 000
less: Sales (at cost)			12 000
Closing stock			1 000

Exhibit 3.12

Nicki has sold £12 000 worth (at raw material prices) of goods so this is the direct cost attributable to those sales. Note that she now has stock of £2 000 comprising £1 000 raw materials and £1 000 finished goods. This stock would be included on the balance sheet as a current asset. She has no work in progress.

Overheads are calculated according to when the resources are used, not when cash is paid. For example, rent of £12 000 for a two-year period could be paid in advance; the profit and loss account for the first year will include rent of £6 000 as only that amount is attributable to the first period.

3. *Depreciation is always included in the profit and loss account.* Depreciation does not involve the receipt or payment of cash; it is a book entry. Depreciation is charged in the profit and loss account to show that the use of fixed assets is one of the costs of generating income. It is an allocation of the cost of the fixed assets over their useful, or income generating, lives. It is important, however, that money is put on one side. Otherwise you may not have the resources available when you do need to replace the equipment.

4. *Capital introduced by the owners is not shown on the profit and loss account.*

The overall picture

By looking at Young & Co's Brewery plc statement of profit and loss (see Exhibit 3.13) and a balance sheet (see Exhibit 3.14) for 1990, we can see the previous points in the context of actual financial statements. Whilst Young's is a relatively large business it has a substantial number of employee shareholders and presents its accounts in an extremely simple manner.

As you can see, on a turnover of £52m it generated a trading profit of £5m (10 per cent). It regards raw materials, consumables and beer duty as direct costs, so its gross profit was £33m.

The profit was distributed to cover loan interest, tax and dividends with £1.5m retained in the business for reinvestment.

Young's balance sheet is set out to show 'what they own' (fixed and current assets), 'what they owe' (current liabilities), the net worth and 'how the money was created' (capital employed). Read Young's explanation of all the figures.

Accounts for the self-employed

Accounts for sole traders and partnerships will, in general, be set out in exactly the same way as described above.

In both cases, the total profit is attributed to the sole trader or partners and it is this on which they are taxed. The money drawn out during the year (drawings) is simply an advance against the profit. Some of this profit will have to be reinvested.

The accounts of a partnership include a 'capital account' which summarises their respective 'share' of the business.

The capital account shows how much each of the partners contributed to the business, adds their share of the profit for the year, deducts their drawings and, therefore, their closing capital or share of the equity. This will also take into account any extra capital provided by the partners during the year. (See Exhibit 3.15.)

What are the small company disclosure requirements?

If you are a sole trader or partnership you are not obliged to show your accounts to anyone (except the Inland Revenue and the VAT inspector). As was mentioned earlier, companies have to file their accounts with Companies House. They are then available for anyone to look at and, perhaps, gain useful information about the market-place and specific competitors. Small companies are allowed, however, to file a modified statement of account which is, in reality, simply a balance sheet. (See Exhibit 3.16.)

	Teamwork at Youngs		This Year's Results
	1990	1989	
Turnover	£51,979,661	£45,900,295	Sales of beer, wines and spirits to the trade, sales over the bar in our managed houses, rents from properties we own, royalties and export sales.
Raw materials and consumables	£11,620,991	£10,478,471	Malt, hops and sugar of the finest quality for brewing our traditional beers and prize-winning lagers, finished goods such as wines, spirits and beers from other producers and manufacturers.
Beer duty	£6,881,446	£6,966,801	The tax paid to the Government on production of our beers.
Employment costs	£14,610,508	£12,952,673	The reward for our labour; wages, salaries and pension schemes for our employees both in the brewery and in managed houses.
Profit sharing	£344,436	£321,367	All brewery employees become members of the profit-sharing scheme after five years' service. A one-part share this year is £1,034.34.
Depreciation	£2,286,938	£2,012,291	Plant, machinery, vehicles and pub fittings wear out. Depreciation provides for their replacement.
Other operating costs	£10,843,258	£8,383,883	All the other costs of running the brewery and managed houses: heat, light, power, water, rates, repairs and maintenance; and all the other expenses involved in running the company.
Trading profit	£5,392,084	£4,784,409	THE RESULT OF THIS YEAR'S TEAMWORK AT YOUNGS
PLUS Profit on sale of properties	£298,497	£799,735	
LESS Interest payable	£1,069,971	£751,119	The cost of borrowing money.
Exceptional items		£211,964	There were no exceptional items this year.
Tax	£1,511,006	£1,831,000	Corporation tax for the Government.
Dividends	£1,539,405	£1,377,477	Payment to shareholders for their investment in the company. The Ram Brewery Trust owns 19% of the company.
This year's profit left in the company	£1,570,799	£1,412,604	FOR REINVESTMENT IN THE FUTURE

Exhibit 3.13   Profit and loss account (*Source:* Young & Co's Brewery plc: Report and Accounts 1990)

Exhibit 3.14 Balance sheet (*Source:* Young & Co's Brewery plc: Report and Accounts 1990)

Profit & Loss Account

Sales	70 000
Overheads	20 000
Net profit	50 000
Divided as follows:	
Smith	25 000
Jones	25 000
	50 000

Balance sheet

Fixed assets		110 000
Current assets	16 000	
Current liabilities	5 000	
Net current assets		11 000
Long-term liabilities		40 000
		81 000

Capital accounts

	Smith	Jones
Opening capital	35 000	40 000
Share of profit	25 000	25 000
	60 000	65 000
less: Drawings	22 000	22 000
Closing capital	38 000	43 000

Exhibit 3.15   Partnership accounts

An example of a modified accounts balance sheet is shown in Exhibit 3.16. As can be seen, it gives away little information about the business. It can be deduced that the business made a profit, retained in the business, of £1 032, i.e. the improvement in the revenue reserve. You can do some limited ratio analysis, but the modified accounts give away little else.

Balance sheet at 30 April 1990

		1990		1989
		£		£
TANGIBLE FIXED ASSETS		2 685		2 973
CURRENT ASSETS				
Debtors and prepayments	7 320		6 264	
Cash at bank & in hand	1 093		1 206	
	8 413		7 470	
CURRENT LIABILITIES				
Creditors & accrued charges	2 470		2 847	
NET CURRENT ASSETS		5 943		4 623
		8 628		7 596
FINANCED BY:				
Share capital		10 500		10 500
Loans		1 000		1 000
Revenue reserve		(2 872)		(3 094)
		8 628		7 596

We have relied upon the exemptions for individual financial statements contained in sections 247 to 249 of the Companies Act 1985 because, under that Act, the company is entitled to benefit from those exemptions as a small company.

Source: Patently Aware Ltd

Exhibit 3.16 Modified accounts balance sheet

Basic financial statements: conclusion and checklist

This chapter has introduced two of the key financial statements: the *profit and loss* and the *balance sheet*. In the next chapter we will be looking at techniques for interpreting accounts in more detail. However, by now you should be able to pick up the final accounts for any business and determine:

- The profitability of the business.
- The capital employed and from where it has come.
- The minimum level of working capital required.
  How much money is needed to finance stock and debtors?
- Whether the business is liquid.
  How much of the current assets is held as cash, or easily turned into cash?
- Whether the business is solvent.
  Do the current assets exceed the current liabilities?
  Do the total assets exceed the current liabilities?
  Do the assets exceed the total liabilities?

Exercise

Look once again at the financial statements for Young's Brewery. Then answer the following questions:

1. What is the level of current assets at Young's?
2. How much money is needed to finance stock and debtors?
3. What are the current liabilities?
4. Do the current assets exceed the current liabilities?
5. Is the business solvent?
6. Is the business liquid?

4 Interpreting accounts

Introduction

The previous chapter explained how to read a profit and loss account and a balance sheet. However, it is only when you start to look at the figures closely that they begin to reveal a true picture of the business. By the end of this chapter, you should be able to interpret accounts and to determine whether a business is profitable, liquid and solvent.

Why are trends important?

This chapter primarily looks at the use of financial ratios to interpret accounts. A ratio is simply a relationship between two numbers. Ratios enable you to reduce the information in accounts to a manageable size. They indicate how the business is performing and provide information, trends and patterns. They can be compared to the same ratios in:

1. Previous years' accounts; and
2. The accounts of other companies in a similar line of business.

Ratios provide no information by themselves. But when compared to other ratios they may indicate trends which show that the business is healthy or suggest that remedial action is required. It is normal to look for performance within a range rather than aiming at specific figures.

When looking at financial statements it is rare to take into account the way that purchasing power changes. When comparing year on year figures, this probably does not matter too much. But if you have equipment bought some years ago and which now has lower levels of depreciation this might cause problems. A business which had acquired assets when prices were lower would have lower assets than a business which had acquired its assets more recently. Care must be taken over the interpretation of some ratios and the effect of external factors. For example, a business might increase its sales by 10 per cent. On the face of it this looks good, but if inflation for the period was 15 per cent then it is actually a reduction in sales in real terms. If, say, 20 per cent extra capital has been introduced then an increase in sales of 10 per cent also looks poor.

If you are particularly interested in the ratios of other businesses as part of financial vetting before offering credit, consider how accurately their balance sheet reflects their business. Retailers, for example, often have year ends early in the calendar year – stocks are low after Christmas, debtors have paid and their new stock has not yet arrived. It helps with stock-taking, but also increases their cash and decreases their current liabilities, perhaps giving more favourable results.

Ratio analysis

There are four types of ratios which are often considered important:

1. *Liquidity* – How much working capital is available in the business?
2. *Solvency* – How near is bankruptcy?
3. *Efficiency* – How good is the management?
4. *Profitability* – How good is the business as an investment?

We will look at each of these types of ratio in turn and suggest typical targets.

Exhibit 4.1 shows a profit and loss account and a balance sheet for Katie's Kitchens. This business carries out sub-assembly and installation. As a result, its raw material stocks are relatively small. Note that all the loans and creditors have been shown as current liabilities.

Note, also, that the profit and loss account shows net profit before interest as well as before tax and dividends. This is often known as profit before interest and tax (PBIT). The tax and dividends have yet to be paid, so they are shown as current liabilities. When they are paid, the bank balance will clearly reduce by a similar amount. The level of interest paid and the tax rate are outside the control

Profit & Loss Account

	1989		1988	
Sales	1 100 000		750 000	
less: Direct costs	550 000		375 000	
Gross profit		550 000		375 000
Overheads	370 000		280 000	
Net profit		180 000		95 000
Interest		25 000		24 000
Taxation		38 750		17 750
Dividends		15 000		
Retained in business		101 250		53 250

Balance Sheet

Fixed assets		85 000		56 000
Current assets				
Stock	45 000		25 000	
Debtors	180 000		150 000	
Cash at bank	73 000		35 000	
		298 000		210 000
Current liabilities				
Loans	45 000		75 000	
Creditors	64 750		50 000	
VAT	20 000		25 000	
Dividends	15 000		0	
Tax	38 750		17 750	
		183 500		167 750
Net current assets		114 500		42 250
Net assets		119 500		98 250
Represented by:				
Shareholders' capital	45 000		45 000	
P & L account	101 250		53 250	
Reserves brought forward	53 250			
		199 500		98 250

Exhibit 4.1 Katie's Kitchens

of the business, so consistent use of PBIT gives a fairer indication of how the business is performing.

It was explained earlier that a ratio is a relationship between two numbers. Often, ratios are shown in the format 1:2. In other words, the second amount is twice the first. The same information can be presented by dividing one number by the other, in this case to give 0.5 or turned into a percentage, 50 per cent. In this chapter, all ratios will be shown as a single number and, occasionally, turned into a percentage where that is likely to be a more helpful way to present the information.

Liquidity ratios

A business should always have enough current assets (e.g. stock, work in progress, debtors, cash in the bank, etc) to cover current liabilities (e.g. bank overdraft, creditors, etc). Liquidity ratios are a group of measures relating to working capital which indicate the ability to meet liabilities with the assets available. The current ratio shows the relationship of current assets to current liabilities.

$$\text{Current ratio} = \frac{\text{Current assets}}{\text{Current liabilities}}$$

This ratio should normally be between 1.5 and 2. Some advisers advocate that the current ratio should be at least 2 on the basis that half the assets might be stock. However, if the ratio is much more than 2 you probably have too much liquid cash. If it is less than 1 (i.e. the liabilities exceed the current assets) you could be insolvent. It may, of course, be possible to sell fixed assets to cover your liabilities but you cannot rely on receiving their book value. A stricter test of liquidity is the quick ratio or acid test. Some current assets, such as work in progress and stock, may be difficult to turn quickly into cash. Deducting these from the current assets gives the quick assets.

$$\text{Quick ratio} = \frac{\text{Quick assets}}{\text{Current liabilities}}$$

The liquidity ratio should normally be around 0.7–1. To be absolutely safe, the quick ratio should be at least 1. However, once again, if it is much greater than 1 you probably have too much liquid cash. If it is less than 0.7 you could be insolvent.

$$\text{Current ratio} = \frac{298\ 000}{183\ 500} = 1.6$$

$$\text{Quick ratio} = \frac{253\ 000}{183\ 500} = 1.4$$

Exhibit 4.2   Katie's Kitchens

As you can see in Exhibit 4.2, Katie's Kitchens has a current ratio of 1.6 and a quick ratio of 1.4. They are nearly the same because the stock is only a small proportion of the current assets.

You will recall in the last chapter that it was stated that liabilities due after more than one year are often shown separately. Normally, liabilities such as these will be term loans from the bank or charges for HP or lease purchase. Look at Exhibit 4.3. You will note that this is the same balance sheet as shown in Exhibit 4.1. But £15 000 of the liabilities is, in fact, not due for more than 12 months. As you would expect, this also affects the current and quick ratios which have now become 1.8 and 1.5 respectively. It is not too important where you choose to put the long-term liabilities, provided that you are consistent.

Balance Sheet			
Fixed assets		85 000	56 000
Current assets			
Stock	45 000		25 000
Debtors	180 000		150 000
Cash at bank	73 000		35 000
		298 000	210 000
Current liabilities			
Loans	30 000		55 000
Creditors	64 750		50 000
VAT	20 000		25 000
Dividends	15 000		0
Tax	38 750		17 750
		168 500	147 750
Net current assets		129 500	62 250
Total assets less current liabilities		214 500	118 250
Creditors – amount falling due after 1 year		15 000	20 000
Net assets		199 500	98 250
Represented by:			
Shareholders' capital	45 000		45 000
P & L account	101 250		53 250
carried forward	53 250		
		199 500	98 250

$$\text{Current ratio} = \frac{298\ 000}{168\ 500} = 1.8$$

$$\text{Quick ratio} = \frac{253\ 000}{168\ 500} = 1.5$$

Exhibit 4.3 Katie's Kitchens

Remember that ratios are only a guide; they do not necessarily tell the whole story: business A has a current ratio of 2; business B has a current ratio of 1. Which one is in the better position? On the face of it, business A is in a better position. But consider these figures:

Business A

Liabilities		Assets	
Creditors	10 000	Debtors	15 000
Overdraft	5 000	Stock	15 000
	15 000		30 000

Current ratio = 2

Business B

Liabilities		Assets	
Creditors	30 000	Debtors	5 000
		Cash	25 000
	30 000		30 000

Current ratio = 1

Although business B has considerably higher creditors, they are unlikely all to demand payment at the same time, and the business has a substantial level of cash available. Business A, on the other hand, needs debtors to pay or to liquidate stock before he can pay off any creditors, or reduce his overdraft.

Some analysts find it helpful to calculate the 'defensive interval'. This is the best measure of impending insolvency and shows the number of days the business can exist if no more cash flows into the business. It is industry-prone and depends on profit margins in the industry. As a guide, it should be 30–90 days.

$$\text{Defensive interval (days)} = \frac{\text{Quick assets}}{\text{Daily operating expenses}}$$

$$\text{Defensive interval} = \frac{253\,000}{2\,468} = 103 \text{ days}$$

Exhibit 4.4 Katie's Kitchens

Solvency ratios

If the net worth of the business becomes negative, i.e. the liabilities exceed the assets, then the business has become insolvent. In other words, if the business closed tomorrow it would not be possible to satisfy all the people who are owed money. Allowing your business to become insolvent is now an offence, so you should take care to watch the figures closely.

One ratio which gives an indication of solvency is the gearing. This is a term often used by financiers. Gearing is defined in different ways by different analysts. We will define it here as the ratio of debt (i.e. loans from all sources including debentures, term loans and overdraft) to total finance (i.e. shareholders' capital plus reserves plus long-term debt plus overdraft). The higher the proportion of loan finance, the higher the gearing.

A debenture is a form of loan finance more often found in large businesses than in small ones. Debentures are considered long-term debt.

$$\text{Gearing} = \frac{\text{Debentures} + \text{Loans} + \text{Bank overdraft}}{\text{Total long-term financing plus bank overdraft}}$$

The gearing should not be greater than 50 per cent, although it often is for new, small businesses. The average is 40 – 50 per cent. It should be as high as possible without being so high as to cause bankruptcy. In other words, have as high a proportion of debt as you can get away with. This will also give a higher return on the capital employed. Interest is tax deductible so debt is cheap compared to equity, although it may hurt your cashflow more. If cashflow is stable and profit is fairly stable, then you can afford a higher gearing. (Preference shares are normally considered as part of fixed interest debt rather than equity.)

In addition to watching the gearing, financiers will also want to be satisfied that you will be able to pay the interest on their loans. They particularly look, therefore, at how many times your profit exceeds their interest.

$$\text{Interest cover} = \frac{\text{Profit before interest and tax}}{\text{Interest}}$$

If this is more than 4 it is very good. If it is less than 2 it may indicate problems ahead.

$$\text{Gearing} = \frac{45\ 000}{244\ 500} = 0.18$$

$$\text{Interest cover} = \frac{180\ 000}{25\ 500} = 7$$

Exhibit 4.5 Katie's Kitchens

Efficiency ratios

Efficiency ratios provide a measure of how much working capital is tied up, indicate how quickly you collect outstanding debts (and pay your creditors) and show how effective you are in making your money work for you.

Probably the most important efficiency ratio to worry about initially is the debtors' turnover ratio and your average collection period. The debtors' turnover ratio is the number of times the total outstanding debt is turned over, usually in a year.

$$\text{Debtors' turnover ratio, d} = \frac{\text{Sales during year}}{\text{Average debt over year}} = \frac{\text{Sales}}{(D_1 + D_2)/2}$$

D_1 and D_2 represent the debtors at the beginning and the end of the period. Adding together and dividing by two thus gives the average debtors for the period. If the period is a year, dividing this ratio into the days of the year gives the average collection period in days.

$$\text{Average collection period of debts} = \frac{365}{d} = n \text{ days}$$

If you are monitoring your debts carefully on a monthly basis, then you could substitute monthly figures.

$$d = \frac{\text{Sales during month}}{(D_1 + D_2)/2}$$

$$\text{Average collection period} = \frac{30}{d} = n \text{ days}$$

Debtors' turnover ratio, $d = \dfrac{1\ 100\ 000}{165\ 000} = 6.7$

Average collection
period =   55 days

Exhibit 4.6   Katie's Kitchens

Credit control is an important aspect of financial management. You should aim to keep this collection period as short as possible. Do you know the typical average collection period for your business sector? Many businesses think they operate on 30 days, but often find it is worse than that. As a rule of thumb, your working capital requirements should be equal to your daily turnover multiplied by your collection period in days. A £10 000 per month turnover (say, £400 per day) with a 60-day collection period requires £24 000 of working capital. If you do not have this amount of cash handy, then you need it as an overdraft facility.

Monitoring how long it takes to pay your suppliers is as important as knowing how long your customers take to pay you. If suppliers have to wait too long, they may withdraw credit facilities.

$$\text{Creditors' turnover ratio} = \frac{\text{Sales}}{(C_1 + C_2)/2}$$

As with the debtors, C_1 and C_2 represent the creditors at the beginning and end of the period. Adding and dividing by two gives the average creditors for the period. A similar format is used for other efficiency ratios. Once again, you can divide this number into 365 to give your average payment period.

Creditors' turnover ratio, $c = \dfrac{1\ 100\ 000}{57\ 375} = 19.2$

Average payment period = 19 days

Exhibit 4.7   Katie's Kitchens

Although it is not the case in this example, business people often try to match their payment period to their collection period.

You will also need working capital to hold stock of raw materials. Stock will naturally increase in times of expansion, and decrease in times of contraction. For some businesses, such as wholesalers and some retailers, a high stock turnover ratio is essential in order to make any profit. A low stock turnover could indicate the presence of dead stock, which should be disposed of rapidly.

It is conventional to use sales in the stock turnover ratio, although it is more correct to use purchases (i.e. cost of sales).

$$\text{Stock(s) turnover ratio} = \frac{\text{Cost of sales during period}}{\text{Average stock level during period}}$$

The alternative figure is stock turnover in days (i.e. how many days does it take to turnover the stock). This is, in fact, a similar calculation to payment periods and collection periods. It is suggested, however, that you use 'sales days' rather than 365 to give a more accurate figure.

$$\frac{(S_1 + S_2)/2 \times \text{Sales days}}{\text{Cost of sales}}$$

$$\text{Stock turnover ratio} = \frac{550\ 000}{(25\ 000 + 45\ 000)/2} = \frac{550\ 000}{35\ 000} = 15.7$$

$$\text{Stock turnover} = 15 \text{ days}$$

Exhibit 4.8 Katie's Kitchens

The efficient utilisation of assets is one of the hallmarks of an effectively run business. The capital turnover ratio (also known as the asset turnover ratio) will give some clues regarding whether the business is generating sufficient sales revenue from the assets employed. If it is not satisfactory it can be marked in the plan as an area which requires particular attention. Typically it varies between 1.5 and 2, though it is considerably higher in the example. A high ratio suggests an efficient use of capital assets.

$$\text{Capital (K) turnover ratio} = \frac{\text{Sales}}{(K_1 + K_2)/2}$$

$$\text{Capital turnover ratio} = \frac{1\ 100\ 000}{(199\ 500 + 98\ 250)/2} = \frac{1\ 100\ 000}{148\ 875} = 7.4$$

Exhibit 4.9 Katie's Kitchens

Profit ratios

Do you know whether your business is profitable or do you have to wait until the end of the year, when your accounts are prepared, before you discover how profitable you were last year?

There are a number of simple indicators that you can use. The gross profit margin is one figure to watch closely.

$$\text{Gross profit margin} = \frac{\text{Gross profit}}{\text{Sales}}$$

(NB Multiply by 100 if you wish to express this as a percentage of sales.)

Do you know the margin required to make a net profit? If not, you should calculate it and then regularly compare the actual to the target.

You should also monitor the overall profit margin, though this is harder since the fixed costs are not paid equally every month.

$$\text{Profit margin} = \frac{\text{Profit before charging interest and tax (PBIT)}}{\text{Sales}}$$

Do you know the target for your industry? If not, look at the results of some of your competitors. Can you achieve at least their level of profit margin? In luxury goods, for example, this ratio is typically 15 – 20 per cent.

Some funders will want to know the return on the capital employed. This will give a comparison with what could have been achieved had the same sum of money been put in a building society or invested on the stock market.

$$\text{Return on capital (K)} = \frac{\text{PBIT}}{(K_1 + K_2)/2}$$

Note that this is equivalent to the capital turnover ratio multiplied by the profit margin. That is:

Return on capital = Profit margin × return on capital

$$\frac{\text{PBIT}}{\text{K}} = \frac{\text{PBIT}}{\text{Sales}} \times \frac{\text{Sales}}{\text{K}}$$

Some funders include long term debt in the capital employed figure, whereas others prefer to exclude it.

Gross profit margin $= \dfrac{550\,000}{1\,100\,000} = 50\%$

Profit margin $= \dfrac{180\,000}{1\,100\,000} = 16\%$

Return on assets $= \dfrac{180\,000}{148\,875} = 121\%$

Exhibit 4.10 Katie's Kitchens

Industry averages

It is possible in many industries to discover the typical ratios for the sector. You could acquire the annual reports of a number of companies and calculate them for yourself, or else you can buy reports from the Centre for Interfirm Comparison (CIFC) or from ICC Business Publications Ltd.

CIFC are commissioned by businesses, or sometimes by trade associations, to review typical ratios for a particular sector. Ratios can be grouped together into trees which show how the ratios interrelate. Typically, CIFC would agree those ratios to be reviewed and group them into a tree as shown in Exhibit 4.11. Note that their first three are those that were introduced above. They then break these down further to give a wide range of information about the performance of the businesses reviewed.

They then produce tables showing the performance of companies within the sector and also calculate industry averages, as shown in Exhibit 4.12.

You can then calculate the same ratios for your business and compare yourself to the rest of the sector.

If you cannot afford a CIFC report or there is not one available for your industry then look for ICC Business Ratios, often available

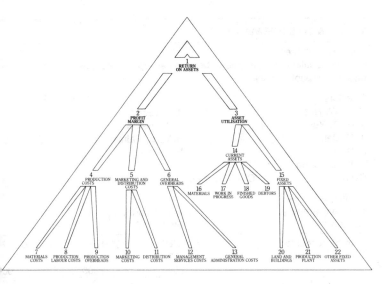

Exhibit 4.11   Tree of ratios (*Source:* Centre for Interfirm Comparison)

TABLE 1 OF 10		Firms											HIGH	AVERAGE	LOW
Ratio		A	B	C	D	E	F	G	H	I	J		HIGH	AVERAGE	LOW
1. Return on Assets	%	25.2	23.9	20.1	19.0	16.7	13.8	12.3	6.7	5.3	4.3		25.2	14.5	4.3
Profit margin on sales and turnover of assets															
2. Profit margin	%	13.1	14.8	13.5	11.7	10.3	9.1	7.7	3.7	3.1	2.9		14.8	9.0	2.9
3. Asset utilisation	times p.a.	1.92	1.41	1.49	1.62	1.43	1.52	1.60	1.81	1.70	1.48		1.92	1.42	1.43
Total costs as a % of sales															
4. Production costs	%	66.5	66.7	65.5	69.1	73.4	68.4	78.4	79.2	81.1	80.1		81.1	72.8	65.5
5. Marketing and distribution costs	%	15.6	13.8	15.9	14.7	11.6	16.3	8.6	11.6	12.1	12.0		16.3	13.2	8.6
6. General overheads	%	4.8	4.7	5.1	4.5	4.7	6.2	5.5	5.5	3.7	5.0		6.2	5.0	3.7
Ratio 2 above	%	13.1	14.8	13.5	11.7	10.3	9.1	7.7	3.7	3.1	2.9		14.8	9.0	2.9
		100.0	100.0	100.0	100.0	100.0	100.0	100.0	100.0	100.0	100.0			100.0	
Production costs as a % of sales value of production															
7. Materials costs	%	67.9	44.6	65.7	48.7	46.3	46.6	49.1	52.1	50.3	40.9		52.1	48.5	44.6
8. Production labour costs	%	10.6	11.1	12.4	13.5	13.5	13.8	14.1	17.7	17.7	14.6		17.7	13.3	10.6
9. Production overheads	%	8.0	11.0	7.7	8.0	13.6	8.5	15.5	13.0	13.1	15.6		15.6	11.4	7.7
Ratio 4 above	%	66.5	66.7	65.5	69.1	73.4	68.4	78.4	79.2	81.1	80.1		81.1	72.8	65.5
Marketing and distribution costs as a % of sales															
10. Marketing costs	%	10.0	9.5	10.7	9.5	7.4	10.1	4.0	7.4	4.8	4.2		10.7	7.9	4.0
11. Distribution costs	%	5.6	4.3	5.2	5.2	4.2	6.2	4.6	4.2	7.3	5.8		7.3	5.3	4.2
Ratio 5 above	%	15.6	13.8	15.9	14.7	11.6	16.3	8.6	11.6	12.1	12.0		16.3	13.2	8.6
General and administration costs as a % of sales															
12. Management services costs	%	1.6	1.7	2.0	1.2	1.4	1.6	1.2	1.2	2.3	1.1		2.0	1.5	1.1
13. General administration costs	%	3.2	3.0	3.1	3.3	3.3	4.6	4.1	4.3	2.4	3.9		4.6	3.5	3.4
Ratio 6 above	%	4.8	4.7	5.1	4.5	4.7	6.2	5.3	5.5	3.7	5.0		6.2	5.0	3.7
Value of assets in £'s per £1,000 of sales															
14. Current assets	%	199	242	251	242	309	288	245	187	240	273		309	248	187
15. Fixed assets	%	322	379	420	375	390	370	380	365	348	403		420	375	322
Total assets	%	521	621	671	617	699	658	625	552	588	676		699	623	521
Current assets in £'s per £1,000 of sales															
16. Materials	%	61	77	75	73	134	88	60	50	65	62		134	74	50
17. Work in progress	%	7	7	10	8	9	12	10	8	15	12		15	10	7
18. Finished goods	%	11	10	15	11	11	18	15	14	15	17		18	14	10
19. Debtors	%	120	148	151	150	155	170	160	115	145	182		182	150	115
Ratio 14 above	%	199	242	251	242	309	288	245	187	240	273		309	248	187
Fixed assets in £'s per £1,000 of sales															
20. Land and buildings	%	187	210	255	211	210	205	191	202	168	180		255	202	168
21. Production plant	%	118	129	145	146	148	141	168	144	150	182		182	147	118
22. Other fixed assets	%	17	40	20	18	32	24	21	19	30	41		41	26	17
Ratio 15 above	%	322	379	420	375	390	370	380	365	348	403		420	375	322

Copyright © The Centre for Interfirm Comparison

Exhibit 4.12   Industry ratio averages (*Source:* Centre for Interfirm Comparison)

from your local library. They produce reports looking at specific markets and provide a considerable amount of information on companies in the sector under review. They also publish Regional Company Surveys which give more limited information about more businesses.

YOUNG & CO'S BREWERY PLC

Principal Activities
Brewing, bottling and the sale of beer, wines, spirits and cider through its public houses.

Directors

C. P. W. Read	J. A Young
J. G. A. Young	C. Clitherow
J. C. Darby	B. D. B. Palmer
J. D. Rose	M. Cotterill
T. ff. B. Young	
Secretary	C. A. Sandland

Trading Address

The Ram Brewery,	Wandsworth,
London	SW18 4JD

	31/03/89	31/03/88	31/03/87
Date of Accounts			
Number of Weeks	52	52	52
	£000	£000	£000
	G	G	G
Sales	45 900	42 816	40 879
Exports	226	236	153
Net Profit Before Tax	4 621	3 594	3 561
Interest Paid	751	595	635
Non-Trading Income	0	1	2
Operating Profit	5 372	4 188	4 194
Depreciation	2 012	1 825	1 533
Trading Profit	7 384	6 013	5 727
Employee Remuneration	11 075	10 100	9 582
Directors' Remuneration	232	219	219
No. of Employees	1 425	1 346	1 298
Fixed Assets	102 162	100 676	99 258
Intangible Assets	0	0	0
Intermediate Assets	527	309	321
Total	102 689	100 985	99 579
Stocks	4 336	4 178	4 174
Trade Debtors	1 627	1 746	1 441
Other Current Assets	1 721	1 110	919
Total Current Assets	7 684	7 034	6 534
Total Assets	110 373	108 019	106 113

Less:			
Creditors	1 819	1 990	3 876
Short-Term Loans	5 624	4 740	1 301
Other Current Liabilities	5 581	4 297	4 346
Total Current Liabilities	13 042	11 027	9 523
Net Assets	97 331	96 992	96 590
Shareholders' Funds	92 466	91 053	90 052
Long-Term Loans	1 503	2 528	3 038
Other Long-Term Liabilities	3 362	3 411	3 500
Capital Employed	97 331	96 992	96 590

Rates of Return			
Return on Capital	4.7	3.7	3.7
Return on Assets	4.2	3.3	3.4
Return on Shareholders' Funds	5.0	3.9	4.0

Profit Margins			
Trading Profit Margin	16.1	14.0	14.0
Operating Profit Margin	11.7	9.8	10.3
Pre-Tax Profit Margin	10.1	8.4	8.7

Turnover Ratios			
Asset Utilisation	41.6	39.6	38.5
Sales/Fixed Assets	0.4	0.4	0.4
Sales/Stocks	10.6	10.2	9.8
Credit Period	13	15	13
Creditors' Ratio	14.5	17.0	34.6
Working Capital/Sales	11.7 –	9.3 –	7.3 –

Liquidity Ratios			
Liquidity	0.6	0.6	0.7
Quick Ratio	0.3	0.3	0.2

Gearing Ratios			
Borrowing Ratio	7.7	8.0	4.8
Equity Gearing	0.8	0.8	0.8
Income Gearing	14.0	14.2	15.1
Total Debt/Working Capital	1.3 –	1.8 –	1.5 –
Debt Gearing	1.6	2.8	3.4
Export Ratio	0.5	0.6	0.4

Source: ICC Publications Ltd

Exhibit 4.13   Young & Co's Brewery plc

Exhibit 4.13 gives an example of information available from the Business Ratios; compare the figures with the Young's annual figures shown earlier. Exhibit 4.14 gives an example of what is available through Regional Company Surveys.

NORTHERN HI-TECH LTD		Incorporated: 15/07/1980		Regd No.	1119999
32-34 St. Martin Street	Secretary:	Principal Activities:			
Darlington	J.W. McGregor	The retail of audio-visual and electrical goods.			
Co. Durham	Directors:				
DL1 1NU	W.A. Williams		£000s	£000s	£000s
Telephone: 0325–555545	J.W. McGinty	Account Date	31/07/89	31/07/88	31/07/87
	S.A. McLintock	Weeks	52	52	52
	B.O. Hoggett				
		SALES	5,782	4,482	6,906
Turnover Range: E		PROFITS	145	270	280
Employee Number Range: S		Total Assets	2,842	1,924	2,213
		Current Assets	2,458	1,770	2,025
Auditors: McGowan & Rodgers		Current Liabilities	1,950	890	1,259
		Return on Capital %	18.5	21.9	24.8
		Profit Margin %	2.5	6.0	4.1
Ultimate Holding Company: American Hi-Tech		Liquidity Ratio	1.3	2.0	1.6
	Corporation				
		Directors Remuneration	350	146	109
Bank: NEWCASTLE LENDERS		Number of Employees	29	20	32
		Average Remuneration (£)	15,517	14,400	12.595
		Sales per Employee (£)	199,379	224,100	215,813

Exhibit 4.14   (*Source:* ICC Publications, Ltd)

Flow of funds analysis

When your annual accounts have been prepared, you have probably found included a statement headed 'sources and applications of funds'. If you cannot find a statement like this in your accounts, get hold of those of a limited company and have a look.

It sometimes seems strange to people who are not accountants that a business can be profitable and yet be short of money or running an overdraft. It must be remembered that profit and cash are not the same. You will recall from the previous chapter that the profit and loss account matches revenues and expenses for a specific period though the revenues accrued for that period may not all have been received. Additionally, some of the expenses may have been pre-paid. Rent and insurance, for example, are typically paid in advance.

The flow of funds statement shows how money flowed into and out of the business during the year, and relates the profit and loss statement to the balance sheet. In particular, it gives a measure of by how much the working capital in the business increased or decreased and can highlight the reasons for the changes. It does not how the amount of working capital available – that is on the balance sheet. Remember that the changes in sources equals the changes in uses. If you spend £5 000 on new equipment, for example, then the uses increase by £5 000. The source might be a bank loan, or retained earnings, but must still be equal to the £5 000 used.

The statement explains:

- The sources of funds;
- The applications for which those funds were used;
- The dependency on external funds;
- The growth (or reduction) of working capital;
- Whether long-term assets are being funded by short-term debt; and
- How the composition of funds has changed.

	Sources of funds	Application of funds
Balance sheet	Liabilities	Assets
Profit & loss account	Revenues	Expenses

Exhibit 4.15   Sources and applications of funds

SOURCE OF FUNDS

Funds generated from operations

i	Profit	XX
ii	Depreciation	XX
iii	Other	XX
		XXX

New long-term funds

iv	Equity	XX
v	Loans	XX
vi	Other	XX
		XXX

Funds from sale of assets

vii	Fixed assets (less accumulated depreciation)	XX
viii	Investments	XX
		XXX

TOTAL SOURCE OF FUNDS   XXXX

APPLICATION OF FUNDS

Purchase of fixed assets

ix	Equipment	XX
x	Buildings	XX
xi	Investments	XX
		XXX

Distribution of profit

xii	Dividends	XX
xiii	Tax	XX
xiv	Other	XX
		XXX

TOTAL APPLICATION OF FUNDS   XXXX

NET SOURCE OF FUNDS   XXXX

THE NET SOURCE OF FUNDS IS REPRESENTED
BY THE FOLLOWING INCREASE IN WORKING
CAPITAL

xv	Stock	XX
xvi	Debtors	XX
xvii	Creditors	XX
		XXX

MOVEMENT IN NET LIQUID FUNDS

xviii	Bank	XX
xix	Cash	XX
		XXX

INCREASE (DECREASE) IN WORKING CAPITAL   XXXX

Exhibit 4.16 Source and application of funds

Source of funds might include profit, sale of equipment, depreciation (although this is a charge to the profit and loss account, it is not a cash outflow), new loans, etc. Applications include losses, purchase of equipment, repayment of loans, increase in net working capital, etc.

Profit as a source of cash is not strictly correct because it includes debtors and creditors, so changes in the level of debtors and creditors are also included.

The total sources of funds always equal the total applications. Any funds not used for the purposes outlined above results in a change in the net working capital.

The typical entries on a flow of funds statement are shown in Exhibit 4.16.

A typical example (taken from Young & Co's Brewery is shown in Exhibit 4.17. Before looking at the example, return to the profit

Sources & application of funds		
Where it came from		
Profit on ordinary activities	4 621 210	
Profit on sale of properties	(298 497)	
Depreciation & adjustments	2 286 338	
Sales of fixed assets	720 895	
Total source of funds		7 329 946
Where it went		
Purchase of fixed assets	8 656 055	
Debentures repaid	266 451	
Dividends	1 477 125	
Taxation	1 802 933	
Total application of funds		12 202 564
Net source of funds		(4 872 618)
Represented by change in working capital		
Increase in stock	213 970	
Increase (decrease) in debtors	(242 146)	
Decrease in creditors	101 344	
Movement in net liquid funds	(4 945 786)	
Increase (decrease) in working capital		(4 872 618)

Source: Young & Co's Brewery plc

Exhibit 4.17 Sources and application of funds

and loss account and the balance sheets for Young's and see if you can produce the flow of funds statement.

As can be seen, Young's working capital has been reduced by nearly £5m. This is primarily because they purchased fixed assets of over £8m. The decrease in working capital has been covered by a decrease in net liquid funds; i.e. money at the bank or held as cash. This is an unusual position to be in. Most businesses, especially small ones, would expect to seek a bank loan to purchase assets. This would increase the source of funds and thus keep the working capital available.

Flow of funds statements can be used to keep an eye on competitors. For example, if firms are spending more on capital equipment than their depreciation charge, they may be expanding. If their working capital has increased it may simply be because of inflation, or poor control of stocks or debtors, or might point to expansion. If working capital decreases, it might be because of a contraction in business, or a trading loss, or it might be because control of stock and debtors has improved. If working capital has decreased, it is likely to lead to a problem of liquidity.

Value added analysis

The price of the products (or service) that you sell represents the costs of the raw materials or services bought in, plus the value that you have added. The added value represents the proportion of overhead costs attributed together with your profit.

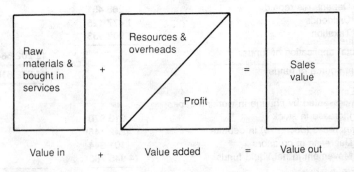

Exhibit 4.18 Value added

The sales price of your product (or service) represents its value to your customers. The value added represents the amount by which your business has contributed to the creation of the country's wealth.

That contribution is shared between four parties: the owners, the employees, reinvestment and the government (through taxes). A profit and loss account concentrates solely on the level of profit and is aimed at shareholders. A value added statement concentrates on the wealth creation and shows its distribution.

Value added can be used as a measure of efficiency. For example, value added per employee is sometimes used to measure the efficiency of labour. Value added/wages gives a measure of staff productivity. Value added/capital employed gives an indication of capital productivity.

Published value added statements are still quite rare, though they are easy to calculate from published accounts. Some companies use them to demonstrate how large a proportion of their income goes to their employees and the government and how little to shareholders.

There are two methods of calculating the added value by a business, both of which, of course, should give the same answer. These are the subtraction method and the addition method. In the subtraction method, all the raw material and bought in service costs are deducted from the total sales. In the addition method, the employment costs, interest, dividend payments, tax, depreciation and retained profit are added together. Look back at the profit and loss account for Young & Co's Brewery. Calculate their value added.

Subtraction method		
Sales during year	51 979 661	100%
less:		
Raw materials etc	11 620 991	22%
All services bought in	10 843 258	21%
Value added	29 515 412	57%

Addition method		
Employment costs	14 610 508	50%
Interest	1 069 971	4%
Dividends & profit share	1 883 841	6%
Tax	1 511 006	5%
Beer duty	6 881 446	23%
Depreciation	2 286 338	8%
Profit retained	1 272 302	4%
Value added	29 515 412	100%

Value added per employee = 19 573		

Exhibit 4.19 Value added statement: Young & Co's Brewery plc

Now look at Exhibit 4.19. Young's have 1 508 employees, so each employee has added value of £19 573.

As can be seen from the example, half the added value goes in employment costs and a further 28 per cent goes to the government

Interpreting accounts: conclusion and checklist

This chapter has introduced a number of ways in which you can analyse the performance of your own business and of others and suggested how you might compare performance. Some performance indicators have been suggested. You should be able to calculate

- Liquidity ratios.
- Solvency ratios.
- Efficiency ratios.
- Profitability ratios.
- Flow of funds statement.
- Value added statement.

Exercise

Turn back to the financial statements for Young's Brewery shown in the last chapter.

1. What is Young's current ratio?
2. How does their current ratio compare with the target?
3. What is their quick ratio?
4. What is their gearing?
5. Why do you think their gearing is so low when their cash position is apparently so poor and their borrowing high?
6. What is Young's profit margin?
7. Now compare your answers with those for Young's prepared by ICC Business Publications (shown in Exhibit 4.13). Is Young's business improving?

5 Business objectives

Introduction

It is important for a business to set objectives. If you do not know where you are going, you will not know when you get there, nor be able to monitor your progress. This chapter explains the importance of setting basic objectives and will help you understand how to prepare budgets and sales targets.

Strategic objectives

Peter Drucker, in his book *The Practice of Management*, argues that the purpose of a business must be 'to create a customer'. What the customer buys and considers to be of value determines what a business is, what it produces and whether it will prosper. In other words, businesses should be market driven. Too many businesses or aspiring business people think they can provide a product, but are unsure of whether it is really needed.

Drucker goes on to argue, therefore, that the two entrepreneurial functions, i.e. the two basic functions of any business, are marketing and innovation. It is appropriate to define your business purpose in terms of your customers and their needs. Many people talk of defining a 'mission statement', though others decide that this is unnecessary. It does help, however, to clarify your thinking if you define the purpose of your business and then to define targets and time-scales. The purpose (or mission) statement should be the overriding factor in guiding your business. It will help you in defining your marketing and will be of immense value when setting financial objectives. Often, though not always, a financial objective is included as part of a company's mission statement.

For example, 'Blooming Marvellous' describes its purpose as follows:

5

'We design, make and market clothes for the fashion-conscious mother-to-be.'

With their production skills they could make clothes for anyone but this statement shows that they have carefully defined their product and marketing strategy.

Many large companies are now publicly quoting mission statements in their annual reports. Northumbrian Water, for example, opens its annual report thus:

'Northumbrian Water Group plc is committed to improving the quality of life, seeking to better its performance to the benefit of its customers, shareholders, its workforce and the environment.'

In setting objectives for the business you may need to satisfy three groups of people, namely: the owners, the staff, and customers. Each will have their own expectations.

1. The owners will be looking for a return on their capital locked up in the business. This may be yours (and your partners') but you should still be aiming for a return better then you would achieve if the money was, say, in the building society. If you have external investors, they will be looking for capital appreciation and evidence that their investment is being well managed.

2. Staff will be looking for realistic rewards for their efforts, career opportunities and an environment in which they are happy to work.

3. Customers will be looking for a product or service which represents good value for money. Customers will only pay premium price for a premium product. You need to take care, therefore, in the positioning of your product in the market place.

Setting overall objectives will be more difficult, therefore, than simply stating that the objective is to operate without making a loss or to maximise profits. Some large companies set themselves targets expressed as ratios – for example, profit per employee, return on equity, profits relative to sales, etc. What is possible will differ between sectors. Capital intensive businesses, such as banks or property companies, may do well on profit per employee, but badly on return on equity. Service sector businesses, with less equity, show a better return on equity, but make less profit per employee. However, remembering that the primary reason for being in business is to make a return on the investment of your time and money, you should set a number of financial and marketing objectives (though marketing objectives are normally translatable into financial ones). These might include, for example:

- Increase in market share.
- Increase in sales.
- Increase in profit.
- Return on investment.
- Improved productivity.

It is often insufficient to set just one of these indicators as an objective. Sir John Harvey Jones, in his book *Trouble-shooters* describes his recommendations for Apricot plc, the computer firm. They had set as an objective 'reaching £500m sales by 1995'. Harvey Jones, however, was anxious that they also set an objective of reaching £50m profit, since simply increasing turnover does not necessarily increase net profit. It may well be easier to run a business with a turnover of £100 000 and 20 per cent net profit than one with a turnover of £200 000 and 10 per cent net profit.

On a smaller scale, one company also in the computer field, set total revenue and gross profit margins for a number of services as shown in Exhibit 5.1. Whilst the numbers are modest they can then be used to monitor the actual results.

Activity	Total revenue	Contribution	Gross profit margin
Sale of goods	20 000	3 000	15%
Adult training	11 300	9 040	80%
Repairs	12 200	5 490	45%
Office services	5 400	3 240	60%
	48 900	20 070	42%

Source: North Tyneside Brass Tacks Ltd: 1987

Exhibit 5.1   Financial objectives

You will need to set long-term objectives for your business, which may include diversification, geographic expansions, market penetration, etc. (Introduce a new product in each of the next three years; have 30 per cent of the local market within six years.) These will then need to be broken down into short-term achievable objectives (increase in market share of 5 per cent per annum). The objectives can then be used to derive performance criteria to measure progress.

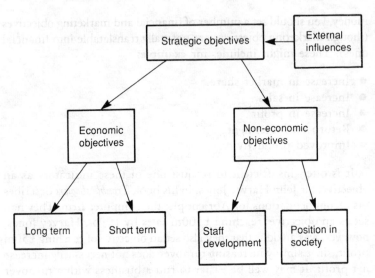

Exhibit 5.2 Setting objectives

As suggested earlier, you may also wish to set some non-economic objectives, particularly regarding staff development. Drucker echoes this thinking. He argues that there are eight key areas in which objectives should be set and against which performance should be measured. These are:

- Market standing.
- Innovation.
- Productivity.
- Physical and financial resources.
- Profitability.
- Manager performance and development.
- Worker performance and attitude.
- Public responsibility.

Once the strategic objectives have been set, it is possible to define the operational objectives which, in turn, leads to the budget. The budget defines the plan or road-map for the business, but it also gives the information needed for effective control.

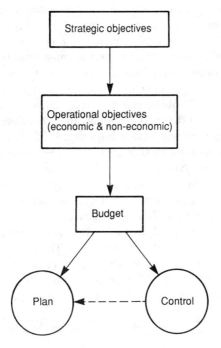

Exhibit 5.3 Planning

Operational objectives

It is very easy for managers in businesses to adopt systems or mechanisms which they think will improve their ability to manage. Remember that management is about handling people and that any system can only provide some support.

Unless you are working on your own, therefore, you need to build your staff into a team who are all pulling in the same direction for the good of the business. Each person must have a job that is directed towards fulfilling the objectives of the whole business.

The aim, in management by objectives, is to agree mutually a set of objectives for every person in the business. These need to be precise ('increase your sales by 5 per cent in volume', rather than 'increase sales'), challenging and achievable. If the targets are unrealistic then people will not even try; on the other hand, people need to be stretched. These objectives then become the yardstick by which individual performance can be measured.

Remember that the human aspect is very important. The following pointers may help in reaching agreement for the business objectives.

1. *Individual responsibility and individual accountability is essential.* Each department or activity must be the sole responsibility of just one person. This avoids buck-passing or confusion as to who is responsible. Moreover, that person must have the authority to exercise control. Responsibility and authority go hand in hand.
2. *If individuals are to work to a plan, they must feel committed to that plan.* They will only be committed if they were consulted in the initial stages. If they had the opportunity to influence the original plan, then they will have a high degree of commitment to the outcome. As stated earlier, all targets must be achievable.
3. *Normally, each person is responsible for controlling some small part of the total.* It can be a great help if every individual is aware of how their part interacts with the remainder, and why failure in one area (theirs) will affect others.
4. *Each person can only do so much.* Their efforts should be focused where they will yield the greatest result. There is a very real danger of trying to exercise too much control over too many things. The principle of management by exception (i.e. looking for variances from expectations, and aiming to make corrections), is a sound one.
5. *Ensure individuals are made aware of the results of their efforts.* Praise regularly.

Budgeting

Once the financial objectives have been set, it is possible to prepare and agree a budget. Budgets are generally only set for the short term – say, to the end of the next financial year. The starting point is the sales forecast – how many products at what price, where and when. This can then be turned into a sales budget. Remember that a budget is not a forecast. Although it is based on forecasts, it is your target. You are committing the business to perform to that standard. It should, therefore, be achievable but challenging, just as with the objectives for measuring individual members of staff.

Once the sales budget has been prepared it is possible to produce a production budget (direct costs) and a resources budget (overhead costs). These can be combined to give a cash budget (or cashflow forecast), budgeted capital requirements and a budgeted profit and loss account.

The budget will only be as good as the work you put into it, but it is there to help you manage and control the business. You must

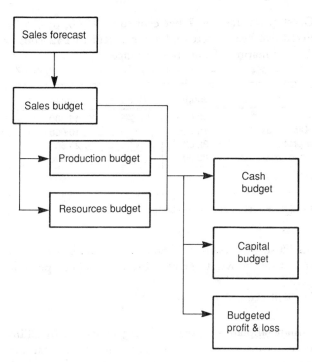

Exhibit 5.4 Budgeting

review it regularly. If the business is going off course, shown by variances from the budget, then you will need to take corrective action. All corrective action needs to be flexible, however. Major changes in one area may alter the performance in another.

Financial aspects

Good financial results will not arise by happy accident. They will arrive by realistic planning and tight expense control. Exhibit 5.5 illustrates the need for tight controls. Remember that profit is the small difference between two large numbers – sales and costs. It follows therefore that a relatively small change in either costs or sales will have a disproportionate effect on profit.

Net profit will disappear under the following conditions:

1. Sales fall by 5 per cent, i.e., gross profit falls to £29 600 and a net profit becomes a net loss; or

2. Gross profit falls by 7 per cent to £29 760; or
3. Fixed overheads increase by 7 per cent to £32 100; or
4. A combination of the above changes.

	Budget	Change	Actual
Sales	48 000	5%	45 600
less: Direct cost	16 000		16 000
Gross profit	32 000		29 600
Overhead expenses	30 000		30 000
Net profit	2 000		(400)

Exhibit 5.5   Effect of change on budget

In this illustration profit is sensitive to relatively small changes in areas 1. to 4. above. Control is exercised by comparison with a budget.

You will need to produce:

- A financial plan – agreed as being achievable by all involved.
- Some means of monitoring performance against the plan. Monitoring will compare monthly accounting 'actuals' with plan projections. It is essential to have an accounting system capable of providing relevant, up-to-date information.
- Since there will always be differences between the actual and plan, we need some form of control. Beyond a certain organisational size, control can only be exercised by delegation. This is why the human aspect is so important.

Accounting centres

The importance of individual accountability was mentioned earlier. This requires you to delegate authority and responsibility. One way of giving financial responsibility to individuals is to set up a system of accounting centres. (You may have heard the term profit centre and cost centre – inevitably some functions do not make a profit and tend to be scorned by those that do – so a neutral term seems more appropriate.)

Where businesses make a range of more than one product, each product is often split into a separate accounting centre. Not only does this devolve some of the financial responsibility, it also makes it easier to determine which products are profitable. Some costs, such as factory rent, are more difficult to allocate so these are often recorded in a holding account and then split on some arbitrary basis between the different products.

The indirect costs may be allocated, for example, by the proportion of total sales represented by each product (by volume or cost), or by proportion of machine time used, or by some other appropriate method.

Whilst this split will give at least an indication of the profitability of each product, beware of the temptation to cease sales of a particular product because profit is too low or there is an apparent loss. The effect of eliminating one product will be to spread the indirect costs over fewer products; thus, sales of the other products may need to be increased as a result. It is essential, however, to ensure that all products are making a contribution.

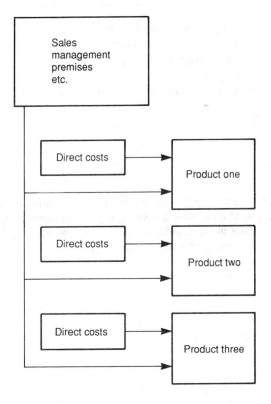

Exhibit 5.6   Cost allocating

We will look further at the effect of this split in the next chapter.

Business objectives: conclusion and checklist

It is important to define:

- The key purpose for your business.
- The strategic objectives to achieve your key purpose.
- Operational objectives to lead towards the strategic objectives.
- Financial objectives.
- A budget (for the business and for individual managers).

There are four essential aspects of budgeting:

- Involve all responsible personnel.
- Produce a viable financial plan.
- Have an accounting system capable of monitoring performance against the plan.
- Have a system of management controls capable of keeping the business on the right track.

Exercise

Sit quietly and think about where you want your business to be in, say, five years' time. How are you going to get there? Once you start to answer those questions, you are well on the way to setting strategic and operational objectives.

6 Costing and pricing

Introduction

Many people have some difficulty calculating the cost for their product or service and let their competitors effectively set the price. By the end of this chapter you will understand how to determine the cost of your product or service and will be able to set a price.

Elements of pricing

You need to charge a price which will cover all your costs and generate a reasonable profit. Remember that there is little relationship between costing and pricing. The price should be the maximum amount that people will pay for your product or service. Costing aims to allocate costs between jobs and periods, to control costs effectively and to minimise the cost of production. One of your objectives should always be to reduce costs and improve productivity. Keeping the price high and the costs low will, therefore, maximise profit.

But you need to know how to spread the costs. If you are manufacturing, how do you spread the costs over the total number of items? If you are offering a service, how do you spread the costs over the total number of hours of service, bearing in mind differing qualities of service during this total? Normally, costs are spread on the basis of volume of production, though over a specific period rather than on an individual job basis.

Defining costs

It is easy to see all the different costs that a business incurs, but it is often helpful to divide these up. You may have heard people talk about direct and indirect costs, fixed and variable costs. Some of these terms are used interchangeably although they should not be.

Variable costs are those that vary in proportion to the level of production. These will include, for example, raw materials, direct labour and sub-contract work. However, some overhead costs, such as use of electricity, may also vary with total production even though they are difficult to allocate directly. Variable costs are sometimes called marginal costs by accountants.

Fixed costs, on the other hand, do not vary in the short term and are not dependent on the level of production. These include rent, rates, insurance, managers' salaries, etc.

Direct costs are those that can be directly attributed to the production of a particular product or service. Raw materials are direct costs. Sub-contract labour is a direct cost. Deducting the direct costs from the sales revenue for a particular product gives its 'contribution' towards overheads and profit.

Indirect costs are the opposite of direct costs – those costs that cannot be directly attributed to a specific product. It can be seen that fixed costs are indirect; variable costs, though, might be direct or indirect.

Most small businesses do not need to worry too much about these definitions. To avoid confusion, therefore, I will use the terms direct costs to cover those costs attributable to a particular product (or service) and overheads to cover all the other expenses of running the business. The overheads are indirect – some will vary with the level of production; some will be fixed. For most small businesses, the overheads can generally be regarded as fixed, at least in the short term.

If you are self-employed (as a sole trader or a partner) the money available to you is the profit, i.e. the sales revenue less all the costs. Naturally, you need to draw money out from the business on a regular basis, but those drawings are simply an advance against profit. Furthermore, you are taxed on the entire profit. For the purpose of calculating costs, however, it probably makes sense to treat your drawings and any income tax as an overhead cost.

If you run a company, then your salary is regarded as a business overhead and you will be paying tax through the PAYE scheme. It should be included as an expense along with all other staff costs. The only extra tax will be corporation tax which is charged on the net profit.

Setting an hourly rate

If you are providing a service, then you will need to know how much to charge per hour. You may also estimate the total time required and offer your customers a fixed price. But your starting point has to be how to calculate an hourly rate. This can be expressed by the following:

$$\text{Hourly rate} = \frac{\text{Business overheads}}{\text{Annual productive hours}}$$

Remember that not all your working hours will be productive – some time will be required for promoting your business, buying supplies, doing the books, etc. You will need some holidays and to allow for illness. In an ideal world, you would set your price once you know what your business overheads will be. Since this is not possible, you have to use your budget figures. Allow a little extra for cost increases during the year and for contingency costs.

6

Catherine provides bespoke fashion garments on an individual basis. Her business has overheads of £10 000. Catherine draws £200 per week and she expects to work 30 productive hours each week for 47 weeks of the year.

$$\text{Hourly rate} = \frac{10\,000 + (200 \times 52)}{(30 \times 47)} = \frac{20\,400}{1\,410} = £14.47 \text{ per hour}$$

Exhibit 6.1 Catherine's Custom Clothes

You can use this method to calculate an hourly rate whether you are providing a service or manufacturing to order, for example, fashion, graphics, etc, where the key element is your time.

Manufacturing cost

If you are manufacturing, then you can calculate a cost per item in a similar way. This time, however, you need to estimate how many items you are likely to sell. Then:

$$\text{Item cost} = \frac{\text{Business overheads}}{\text{Total items}}$$

Peter runs a company which manufactures fresh pasta which he sells to the hotel and health food trade. His annual fixed costs, including his salary are £24 000. After careful market research, he expects to sell 32 000 kilograms of pasta in his first year.

$$\text{Cost} = \frac{24\ 000}{32\ 000} = 75\text{p/kg}$$

Adding raw material costs of 19p/kg gives a total cost of 94p/kg.

Exhibit 6.2   Peter's Pasta

If you make more than one product, you need to split the business overheads between the different products.

There are a number of ways in which you may choose to divide the fixed overheads – on the basis of the volume manufactured of each different product, or the time taken to make each product, or the floor area needed by each production process, or pro rata according to the sales income of each product. It may be appropriate to use a combination.

For example, imagine that you run a business manufacturing three products. Sales and costs are as shown in Exhibit 6.3.

	One	Two	Three	Total
Sales	10 000	20 000	15 000	45 000
Direct costs	5 000	10 000	10 000	25 000
Fixed costs	4 000	8 000	6 000	18 000
Total costs	9 000	18 000	16 000	43 000
Net profit	1 000	2 000	(1 000)	2 000

Exhibit 6.3

The fixed costs are split up between the three in proportion to total sales income, i.e. 40 per cent. As can be seen, product three is apparently making a loss. Should you stop manufacturing this product? Even if you do, the fixed costs will remain fixed so you will still have to recover £18 000. Let's look at the figures in a different way.

If you look at the contribution of each product, you can see that all the products do make a contribution. The total contribution is £20 000 which covers the total fixed costs and leaves a net profit of £2 000. Stopping production of product three would cut £5 000 contribution leaving only £15 000 total contribution and a loss of £3 000.

	One	Two	Three	Total
Sales	10 000	20 000	15 000	45 000
Direct costs	5 000	10 000	10 000	25 000
Contribution	5 000	10 000	5 000	20 000
Fixed costs				43 000
Net profit				2 000

Exhibit 6.4

In this particular case, there may be a more accurate way of splitting the fixed costs in order to set a reasonably accurate price for each product. Rent and rates might be split according to floor area required; advertising might be split pro rata on sales value; product liability insurance might be split pro rata on sales volume; etc.

You might be able to think of all your products as multiples of a basic product. One joinery firm, for example, splits its fixed costs by regarding everything as chairs. Obviously a chair equals a chair. But a table was equal to three chairs, a wardrobe was equal to six chairs, etc. Market research suggested how many of each item might be sold and the fixed costs were allocated accordingly.

How do you derive the total cost?

Once you have determined how to allocate the overhead costs per item or per hour, you are then ready to add the direct costs to give the total cost. Adding an additional profit margin and VAT, if appropriate, provides you with the sales price.

You will, of course, have to compare your price with the competition. If it is higher, do you offer a better quality? If it is lower, are you aiming to position yourself lower in the market-place or could you sell at a higher price and make more profit? If your product is new, or unique, then you might be able to set your price higher, reducing it later when competitors appear.

Let us work through an example.

How should Graham Watts of Graham's Graphics decide how much to charge customers? He could use several approaches, such as the going rate for commercial designers, or charge the most possible while still being cheap enough to attract customers.

On one-off contracts how would he know how much to charge? Each one will be different requiring different material, etc. However, the main problem is how much to charge for one hour of Graham's time. How valuable is he? He must charge enough per hour to ensure he makes a profit.

How could you begin to come to a reasonable figure? From your budget, you have isolated your overheads, i.e. rent, rates, etc – costs that will be incurred whether work is being done or not.

The price Graham needs to charge will be equal to:

$$\frac{\text{Fixed costs} + \text{Annual drawings}}{\text{Annual productive hours}} \times \frac{\text{Direct}}{\text{hours}} + \frac{\text{Material}}{\text{costs}} + \frac{\text{Percentage}}{\text{profit}}$$

If the business is VAT registered then a further 15 per cent would need to be added to the price.

If Graham Watts is the only person working for the firm the business time he charges to jobs in the year must cover all the overheads that the business has.

Overheads for the year:

Rent (12 × £200)	=	2 400
Rates (4 × £150)	=	600
Car (insurance and tax)	=	300
Telephone	=	500
Electricity	=	150
Other (stationery, etc)	=	150
Depreciation	=	500
		£4 600

Graham wishes to take out of the business £10 000 to cover his own personal costs.

Therefore, Graham Watts needs to recover £14 600 by charging out his labour.

He expects to work 47 weeks each year, allowing for four weeks' holidays (including bank holidays) and one week's illness. He expects to have 35 productive work hours each week. He knows he will also have to spend at least one hour each day on average dealing with the accounting records, answering telephone calls, getting new customers, etc, so his total working week is 40 hours. It is only productive hours, though, that he can charge to customers.

Therefore, he expects to work 1 645 hours per year (i.e. 47 weeks × 35 hours).

However, Graham Watts feels he might not have enough customers to fill all his available time. Therefore he decides it would be better if only 75 per cent of the available hours were used in calculating the charge per hour.

That is, Graham believes that, on average, 25 per cent of the time he will be available to do jobs but will have no work to do.

Therefore, his productive number of hours per year = 1 645 × 75% = 1 234 hours.

His hourly rate, therefore, will be: $\frac{14\ 600}{1\ 234}$ = £11.83

For each job, Graham will estimate how long it is going to take and then quote a price incorporating a rate of £11.83 per hour.

It will also be necessary to charge materials used on the job. To ensure all material costs are fully recovered, it is normal practice to quote something like cost plus 10 per cent.

Thus, if a contract is going to take six hours and involve expenditure on materials of £20 then a price to quote would be:

```
6  × 11.83 = 70.98
20 ×  1.1  = 22.00
              92.98
```

If Graham wants the business to grow, he will need more profit so that he has spare money to reinvest. If he is looking for £10 000 net of tax, he will have to make more profit to pay the tax bill. This means he will either have to charge more per hour, or find more work to fill some of the other hours he has available.

If Graham's Graphics is registered for VAT, he would then have to add a further 15 per cent to his price.

Break-even analysis

Once you know your costs and estimated selling price, then you are in a position to calculate how many products, or hours of your time, you need to sell to break-even, i.e. to cover all your costs. Any further sales then provide you with a profit. The easiest way to do this is to draw a graph, showing your costs and income.

First show the overhead costs. For most small businesses, it is reasonable to assume that these are fixed for the year no matter what volume of product you manufacture or how many hours service you sell. The overhead costs will therefore be shown as a horizontal line. For some businesses, this is an over-simplification. For example,

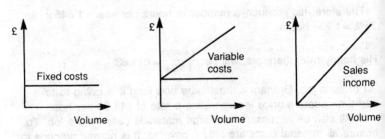

Exhibit 6.5 Break-even

production beyond a certain volume will require bigger premises or more equipment.

After plotting the fixed costs, draw a line to show the variable costs. These are added to the fixed costs to show the total cost for a given level of production. Again, this is a simplification. You might, for example, attract discounts for buying raw materials in larger volumes. Lastly, plot your income graph. This starts from the origin since no sales means no income. The sales line shows how much income you will generate selling at a particular price.

These can now be combined into a single break-even chart. The point where the sales income equals the total costs shows your break-even point. A higher price will give a break-even point after fewer sales, but can you sell at that price? A lower price may attract more customers, but will you cover all the costs?

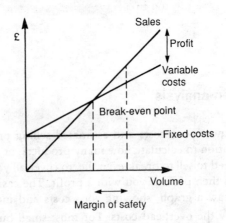

Exhibit 6.6 Break-even

The higher above break-even that a business can operate, the greater its margin of safety.

Absorption costing

The costing method shown above has simply demonstrated one way of allocating overhead costs to your product or service. If you have more than one product or service, then the difficulty arises of how the overheads should be allocated, as discussed earlier.

A slightly different way of achieving the same answer is absorption costing. In absorption costing, no distinction is made between direct and overhead costs – they are all absorbed into the cost of the product. If you make more than one product, you still have the problem of deciding how to allocate the overhead expenses across your product range. For the sake of simplicity, let us look at an example of a business that only makes one product.

You need to calculate the entire costs to the business for a given level of production. These costs are then plotted on a graph as shown in Exhibit 6.7. Now choose a selling price, say, £200. From the graph, you can see that the break-even point is sales of 500 doors.

Daniel makes wooden garage doors. His overhead costs are £50 000 per annum. The direct costs, for wood and paint, are £100 per door.

If he makes 100 doors during the year, the total costs are £60 000 (i.e. £100 × 100 doors + £50 000) giving a cost per door of £600. If he makes 200 doors, the total cost is £70 000 giving a cost of £350 per door. For 500 doors the total cost is £100 000 but the cost per door has dropped to £200.

Each of these are the break-even figures which can be plotted on a graph.

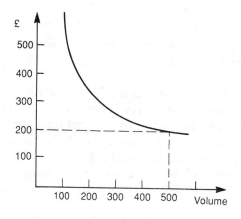

Exhibit 6.7 Daniel's Doors

If your production capacity is restricted to 400 doors, then each must be sold at £225 to break even. A higher price for the same number of sales will generate a profit.

Modern, computerised spreadsheet packages make production of graphs such as this simple and straightforward.

Marginal costing

The marginal cost of a product is the extra cost of producing one more unit. Whilst the marginal cost is probably, for the small business, just a direct cost, it may include some overhead costs. The marginal cost can then be compared to the marginal revenue, i.e. the additional contribution from one extra sale can be calculated.

Clearly, the marginal cost must be set in the context of existing production. The cost of increasing production from 300 doors to 301 may be just the material costs. But if the capacity is 400, the cost of increasing production to 401 may include new premises, new equipment, extra staff, etc.

No attempt is made to allocate overhead costs to production. The contribution from each sale is simply a contribution to overheads. Once all the overheads are covered, then it becomes a contribution to profit.

		Per unit
Sales	10 000	20
Direct costs	4 000	8
Variable costs	1 000	2
Contribution	5 000	10

Exhibit 6.8 Marginal costing

Look at Exhibit 6.8. The total manufacturing cost per widget is £10 – i.e. the direct costs of raw materials and the allocation of variable overheads (such as electricity and transport). The sales income per extra widget is £20, so the contribution is £10. For each extra widget the marginal cost is £10. Provided these can be sold at any price over £10, then it is worthwhile doing so since they generate extra contribution towards the fixed costs – or towards profit.

As can be seen, the main difference between absorption costing and marginal costing is in the treatment of the fixed overheads.

Absorption costing is normally preferred for manufacturing costs. It can be used to help:

- Control expenditure.
- Set a sales price.
- Value stock correctly (if the stock is revalued to take account of the added value).

Standard costing

One method of costing often used by larger manufacturers is known as 'standard costing'. The standard cost is the total cost of direct labour, direct costs and a suitable proportion of the variable overhead costs incurred in the production process.

This requires the calculation of a standard time to produce the article. For highly mechanised production it might be appropriate to use machine hours; otherwise use labour hours. The cost of labour for that length of time can then be deduced. The variable costs can be attributed, either split by the standard time or by volume. The direct costs can then be added.

The main advantage of a costing system like this is that the requirement for a series of standards gives at least some criteria for measuring staff performance.

In Chapter 4, the importance of monitoring financial ratios was discussed. There are a number of other ratios which can also be monitored:

1. $\text{Efficiency ratio} = \dfrac{\text{Standard hours}}{\text{Actual hours}}$

If a widget is expected to take a standard time of six hours to manufacture and actually takes eight hours, then the efficiency ratio is 6/8 or 0.75 (i.e. 75 per cent).

2. $\text{Activity ratio} = \dfrac{\text{Actual standard hours}}{\text{Budgeted standard hours}}$

This measures the activity of the business. If you are using standard costs, then knowing how many widgets you intend to make will give you an indication of the total budgeted hours. A business expects to make 100 widgets in a week. At six hours per widget, this will require 600 hours.

In fact, the business works 660 standard hours. The activity ratio is 660/600 = 1.1 or 110 per cent.

3. Capacity ratio = $\dfrac{\text{Actual hours available}}{\text{Budgeted standard hours}}$

If the business has 15 production staff, all of whom work a 40-hour week, there are 600 standard hours available. If the budget requires 600 hours, then the capacity ratio = 1 or 100 per cent. No more work can be done unless the staff can complete the work in less than the standard time (is the standard time correct?) or they can work overtime. Otherwise you will have to recruit more staff or schedule the work for a different week (if possible).

Costing and pricing: conclusion and checklist

In this chapter, we have looked at:

- Defining different types of costs.
- Setting an hourly rate to recover overheads.
- Setting an item rate to recover overheads.
- Break-even analysis.
- Absorption costing.
- Marginal costing.
- Standard costing.

You need to decide the method that is most appropriate to your product or service and one that you are happy to use. Then stick to it. You should continually review:

- The price at which you sell your product or service.
- Your costs – with the aim of reducing them.

Exercises

1. Imagine that you are the owner of a painting and decorating business. You employ five staff in addition to yourself. You expect to undertake 240 jobs next year at an average of six 'person days' per job. Each of your staff costs you £10 000 per

annum (including NI). Your overhead costs are £25 000 pa. You hope to draw at least £20 000 net from the business. How much would you expect to charge for the average job?

Now imagine that you are running a business manufacturing steel filing cabinets. The manufacturing process includes cutting the sheet steel, folding, welding and riveting, assembling (runners, locks, etc) and painting.

From a formal time study and experience, you know that the standard time to complete a cabinet shell is 25 minutes and for one drawer is 30 minutes. Painting requires 30 minutes. Final assembly and packing requires 5 minutes.

(a) What is the total standard time to complete a four-drawer filing cabinet?
(b) If your staff can actually complete a filing cabinet in 2 hours 30 minutes, what is the efficiency ratio?
(c) If you have five staff, who can carry out all the tasks equally well, how many hours' work might you have available in one year?
(d) If the actual number of hours available in a particular week is 130, what is the capacity ratio?

6

7 Formulating the plan

Introduction

Once you have set your overall objectives and the price for your product or service, you are ready to calculate detailed budgets. By the end of this chapter, you will understand how to prepare a financial plan and how to assess your working capital requirements.

The sales forecast

Chapter 5 outlined the process by which a business plan should be derived. Let us now look at that process in more detail. The first requirement is to forecast your likely sales. Do not simply take last year's figure and add 5 per cent or whatever. Look at the total market – is it expanding or contracting? Talk to your customers about their likely use of your product or service next year. What marketing are you planning to attract new customers? If you employ sales people, ensure they bring back market intelligence. If you are already in business, you will almost certainly have some historical data on which you can base your estimate.

You need to estimate your sales both by value and volume. Are you aware of the effect of price on your product? Have you monitored how demand changes with price changes? If not, this is data that you should be aiming to collect in future. You will probably have a record of the sale price for successful sales, but also record the sale price for unsuccessful sales. If possible, discover what prices are being charged by your competitors. Sometimes this is easy; in retail, for example. Sometimes it is more difficult. If you lose a contract, telephone and find out why. Did you lose on price? Did you lose on quality? Did you lose because your delivery date was too slow? This is all useful market intelligence and will help you to build and to maintain an overview of the market. When you win a contract, you should also try to find out why your customers preferred you. Do not take your customers for granted.

For many businesses, it should be possible to construct a price/demand graph (see Exhibit 7.1).

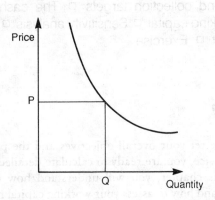

Exhibit 7.1 Demand curve

Economists generally argue that demand is a function of price. As the price of a product falls, the demand increases. Look at how quickly Sony Walkmans or compact disc players became more common once the price started to fall.

Price is not the only function influencing demand. Others include consumers' preferences, perhaps at the present for more environmentally sensitive goods; changes in disposable income; etc.

However, you should be concerned about the 'price elasticity' of your product or service. You want to know how many more or less of your products will be bought if you change the price. This is known as the price elasticity of demand.

As the price rises, the demand falls, but total revenue rises. As the price falls, demand rises, but revenue falls. This does not always happen, of course. You will eventually reach a point where raising your price further leads to a decrease in revenue. Ideally, you would set your price to maximise your revenue. Occasionally (paradoxically) setting higher prices leads to increased sales volume. One of our clients, for example, had such a demand for his product that he did not have the time and resources available to meet it. He was advised to raise his prices to decrease demand (but to keep the revenue at least as high). However, his target audience then perceived his product to be of higher quality and the demand increased!

Nigel offers a high quality photographic service. He charges £10 for an A4 print. If he changes the price to £11, his sales drop from 1 000 units pa to 950 units.

$$\text{Price elasticity, } e = \frac{\text{change in demand}}{\text{change in price}}$$

$$= \frac{50/1000}{1/10}$$

$$= 0.5$$

Exhibit 7.2 Price elasticity of demand

Unless price elasticity is relatively high (i.e. close to 1), sales are not too sensitive to changes in price.

It is also helpful to know the effects of other activities on sales. What is the effect of advertising expenditure, for example? This is often difficult to monitor, especially if you advertise regularly and/or in several different ways. Advertising tends to have a cumulative effect – a series of advertisements is likely to generate more sales than one occasional advert multiplied by the number of inserts. Nevertheless, you should attempt to discover how customers find out about you. Record increases in sales, if any, when you advertise. Only change one advertising variable at a time. If you do this carefully over several months, you should be able to build up an overall picture of the effect of advertising. This, too, can be plotted on a graph for ease of understanding.

Sales may increase simply through the cumulative effect of advertising over a number of years, word of mouth, etc. Plot sales over time – it is then possible to calculate trends by means of moving averages or regression analysis.

If you have just started up, or are introducing a new product, then these techniques will be of little help. On the other hand, you should have some detailed market research to call upon. Watch your competitors. Request copies of their annual reports; these are all filed annually at Companies House and are available for a small fee, for example, from Infocheck. Look at Extel and McCarthy information at your library. Most libraries have, or can obtain, copies of market research reports from Mintel, Key Notes, etc. Some industries and trade associations publish market intelligence. Glenigan, for example, publishes a monthly summary of all major building contracts to help businesses in the construction industry. Most important of all, talk to your prospective customers.

The forecast will also need to take account of current orders and enquiries, competitors' price and market share, proposed marketing strategy, general economic outlook, etc.

You may need to break down your sales forecast by geographic area and by seasonal variation. Once you have prepared your forecast, you are ready to set out your sales budget. The budgeting process is normally carried out just once each year.

The sales budget

You have now determined the number of units that you might be able to sell at a given price broken down by product, area, timing, etc. The sales budget is required to provide overall targets and to enable you to prepare the other budgets.

Volume

| | | Area | | |
Month	USA	Europe	Japan	Total
April	2	1	1	4
May	2	2	1	5
June	10	6	7	23
July	15	10	8	33
Total	29	19	17	65

Value

| | | Area | | |
Month	USA £'000	Europe £'000	Japan £'000	Total £'000
April	34	17	17	68
May	34	34	17	85
June	170	102	119	391
July	255	170	136	561
Total	493	323	289	1 105

Exhibit 7.3 Electron: sales budget

A budget by volume and value is shown in Exhibit 7.3. Normally, sales should be shown on a monthly basis for the year. Only four months are shown in the examples to save space. A new product, for which extensive research has been undertaken, is to be introduced by Electron in the three markets shown. After sales of demonstration systems in April and May, the business predicts its sales will increase as shown.

The systems are manufactured by a sub-contractor to a design and specification provided by Electron. Full systems will sell for £17 000 each. Research suggests that, within limits, the price elasticity is not high and so the price has been set accordingly. The volume budget, therefore, translates to a sales budget by value which is also shown in Exhibit 7.3.

The production budget

Once the sales budget has been determined, you are able to prepare a production budget. This budgets for the direct costs. In Electron's case, they are sub-contracting the manufacture completely. They have decided to build up a small stock of finished goods to be able to supply future demand for demonstration systems. They are, therefore, ordering more from the sub-contractor than they expect to sell in the month. They have assumed that the product is received, tested, completed and shipped to their customers all in the same month.

Units				
Month	Ordered	Received	Sold	Closing stock
March				0
April	5	5	4	1
May	6	6	5	2
June	25	25	23	4
July	35	35	33	6
Total	71	71	65	

Exhibit 7.4 Electron: production budget

Do not forget to include direct labour or other variable costs (such as power, transport, etc) if necessary.

The materials purchase budget

If they were a manufacturing business, the next step after the sales budget would be to look at the raw materials holding and ordering requirements. An example is shown in Exhibit 7.5.

Materials purchase budget

	Matls ordered	matls received	Issued to production	Stock
Opening balance				3 000
April	3 500	3 000	3 500	2 500
May	3 500	3 800	3 500	2 800
June	4 000	2 500	3 500	1 800
	11 000	9 300	10 500	

Exhibit 7.5 Manutron

If there are likely to be delays receiving raw materials after ordering them you will need to hold sufficient raw materials to cover production for the typical period of delay. This ties up working capital so your target should be to keep raw materials to a minimum, aiming for 'just-in-time' stock control. This is discussed further in Chapter 11, together with economic order quantities. Purchasing policy should be reviewed regularly to ensure that you are obtaining value for money from suppliers and that you are paying the lowest possible price consistent with the quality desired.

Once raw materials have been issued to production they become 'work in progress'. Work in progress also necessitates working capital, valued at least at the cost of the raw materials that are now in production. If the manufacturing process is a long one, then the value added at each stage (labour, resources, etc) also has to be financed until the product is sold.

When preparing the production budget, remember to watch for the number of machine hours available, the number of labour hours available, etc. If you exceed your capacity you may have problems. On the other hand, you do not want expensive machinery lying idle. So you should also look at your utilisation rates – if they are too low, can you increase them, perhaps by increasing sales or introducing new products.

The overheads budget

Once the production budget has been prepared, the other costs need to be calculated. If you are in manufacturing, it is likely that these will represent a relatively small proportion of the total costs. On the other hand, if you are running a service sector business, it is likely that the overheads will represent a very high proportion or, indeed, all of the cost.

Grafart is a business offering corporate and industrial design services. They employ three designers and a secretary who also does the financial control and all the administration. They have concluded that it would be difficult to charge their labour as a direct cost and have, therefore, estimated their overheads, all of which are fixed, as follows:

Salaries	60 000
Premises	10 000
Marketing	10 000
Travel and Transport	9 000
Insurance	1 000
Other	3 000
Interest	11 000
Total	104 000

In addition to the trading expenses, allowance also has to be made for depreciation of £5 000. This gives a total overheads budget figure of £109 000.

Exhibit 7.6   Grafart: overheads budget

The production cost budget

You are now in a position to pull together the production budget and the overheads budget into a single production cost budget. If you have more than one product, then you will have a production budget for each product. You will also have variable overheads to add for each product. There is no need to split fixed overheads across products at this point since you are trying to determine the total costs.

On the other hand, if some of the costs have been collected on a product or a departmental basis, then it probably makes sense to keep them separate, even at this stage, provided they are all included.

Let us now pull together the figures for Electron. They have direct costs of £10 200 per unit payable to the sub-contractor. They also have variable overheads of £500 per unit (to cover transport, packaging, etc). Lastly, they anticipate fixed overheads of £240 000 per year (to cover salaries, marketing, premises, etc).

These figures can now all be combined into a production cost budget as shown in Exhibit 7.7.

As can be seen from Exhibit 7.3, total sales, if achieved, will generate revenue of £1.1m. The expenses total £0.84m. Thus Electron should make a net profit of £265 000 for the four-month period. Let us now look at Electron's cash requirements.

Production cost budget

	Sub contract £'000	Variable overhead £'000	Fixed overhead £'000	Total £'000
April	51	3	20	74
May	61	3	20	84
June	255	13	20	288
July	357	18	20	395
Total	724	36	80	840

Exhibit 7.7 Electron

Settlement and collection targets

As you might expect, you should aim to negotiate collection periods as short as possible, though you will find that some industries have fairly standard collection periods. Typically you should expect to wait at least 30 days from invoicing until you are paid. If your product represents a substantial sum of money, aim to seek a deposit, part payment on delivery, etc.

Collection and settlement periods need to be watched carefully for budgetary purposes. The construction industry, for example, typically retains 10 per cent of a contract until the architect has certified the work – this often takes weeks!

Additionally, aim for the longest possible settlement periods. You may find some suppliers impose strict terms of seven days or 28 days. You should aim for your settlement period to be at least as long as your collection period if possible.

The ideal situation, of course, is one where your customers pay on receipt of the goods (e.g. retail) or even up-front (e.g. mail order) and you can negotiate, say, 30 days' settlement period. Your customers' payments then become your working capital.

Electron expects, on average, to hold finished goods for 30 days whilst they are completed, tested, packaged and shipped to the customer. Customers will pay half the invoice on delivery and half after a further 30 days.

Whilst Electron's invoiced sales income is £1.1m for the period their cash receipts are estimated actually to be only £348 000.

Electron has negotiated 30 days credit terms with its sub contractor. Marketing, salaries and other fixed costs are payable every month. Remember also to watch out for quarterly or annual payments (such as telephone, rent, insurance, etc). The variable overheads include carriage from the sub-contractor, carriage to the customer, packaging, etc, and are paid as shown in Exhibit 7.9, the cash budget.

The cashflow forecast

The cashflow forecast, sometimes known as the cashflow budget, summarises the cash position of the business. It reflects the timing of receipts and payments for the period, which are summarised in the 'total' column. The accruals column shows the additional income or expenditure which applies to the period, but which was not received or paid out during it. It does not form part of the cashflow forecast, but will help you to identify debtors and creditors, and provide you with the information to prepare a balance sheet and profit and loss account.

The cashflow forecast should include:

- Receipts of cash from customers.
- Payments for raw materials.
- Payments for all other expenses.
- Drawings and wages.
- Capital expenditure.
- Capital or loans introduced.
- Loan repayments.
- VAT receipts and payments (if VAT registered).
- Tax payments.

It is normal to show all of these items separately. They must be shown in the month in which they will occur, as in Exhibit 7.8.

Note that this design of cashflow forecast has rows to show sales by volume and by value. The cash for these sales is shown in the month it is received. The column headed 'accruals' is available to show any cash still owing at the end of the year. Similarly with expenditure, some bills may have been received but not paid. These amounts can be shown as accruals. This will help in the preparation of profit and loss accounts and balance sheets.

Let us now return to our example, Electron, and look at their expected cash budget. Electron holds the goods for 30 days before delivery to the customer. Goods bought by Electron in April, therefore, are delivered in May. Half the cost is paid in May and half 30 days later. Electron has to pay its supplier in May. And so on.

For: ....

Month	Jan	Feb	March	April	May	June	July	Aug	Sept	Oct	Nov	Dec	Total	Accruals
Sales														
Sales by volume														
Sales by value														
Receipts														
Sales – cash	1 890	2 850	3 660	4 890	5 250	5 680	6 180	6 340	6 680	7 040	7 160	7 480	65 100	
Sales – debtors													5 000	
Capital introduced	5 000												5 000	
Grants & loans	20 320	320	400	320	320	400	320	320	400	320	320	400	24 160	
VAT														
Total	27 210	3 170	4 060	5 210	5 570	6 080	6 500	6 660	7 080	7 360	7 480	7 880	94 260	
Payments														
Raw materials	8 000	1 900	1 900	3 000	3 000	3 000	3 000	3 000	3 000	3 694	3 600	3 600	40 694	
Employee wages & NI													0	
Rent, rates & HLP			750		2 850	750			900		2 850	900	9 000	
Advertising etc	1 200	200								200	200		1 800	
Insurance	650												650	
Transport & packaging	100	100	100	100	100	100	100	100	100	100	100	100	1 200	
Telephone			125			125			125			125	500	
Stationery, postage, etc													0	
Professional fees	100												100	
HP & lease payments													0	
Capital items	14 400												14 400	
Loan repayments	305	305	305	305	305	305	305	305	305	305	305	305	3 660	
Loan interest	166	166	166	166	166	166	166	166	166	166	166	166	1 992	
Bank charges			50			50			50			50	200	
Other	1 000		250			250			250			250	2 000	
Other														
Principals drawings/wages	480	480	480	480	480	480	480	480	480	480	480	480	5 760	
VAT													0	
VAT to C & E														
Total	26 401	3 151	4 126	4 051	6 901	5 226	4 051	4 051	5 376	4 945	7 701	5 976	81 956	
Balances														
Cash increase (decrease)	809	19	−66	1 159	−1 331	854	2 449	2 609	1 704	2 415	−221	1 904	12 304	
Opening balance		809	828	762	1 921	590	1 444	3 893	6 502	8 206	10 621	10 400		
Closing balance	809	828	762	1 921	590	1 444	3 893	6 502	8 206	10 621	10 400	12 304	12 304	

As can be seen, Electron requires substantial working capital in order to meet its budget. This might come from its own resources or the company might need to negotiate a bank loan or an overdraft facility.

It is often helpful when preparing cash budgets initially to ignore any finance that is available from the principals or from a bank. The cashflow forecast then shows the true position of the business. It can then be used to decide if the budget is viable and can be adjusted to reflect the true position.

When preparing budgets, remember to allow for increased costs, for instance, due to inflation or future pay awards. You should also allow contingency sums – for example, for repairs to machinery. If you do need a loan, then you will also need to allow an amount for loan interest. If you use equipment, remember to allow for depreciation. Whilst depreciation is not included in the cash budget, you may need to allow for the replacement or repairs of machinery.

If you have a term loan, the repayments will not figure in your profit and loss account – they are not a business expense – although interest charged is an expense. However, the repayments do need to be included in your cashflow forecast.

	April	May	June	July	Total	Accruals
Receipts:						
Sales		34 000	76 500	238 000	348 500	756 500
Total	0	34 000	76 500	238 000	348 500	756 500
Payments:						
Purchase		51 000	61 200	255 000	367 200	357 000
Marketing	5 000	5 000	5 000	5 000	20 000	
Salaries	15 000	15 000	15 000	15 000	60 000	
Transport	1 250	2 750	7 750	15 000	26 750	8 750
Total	21 250	73 750	88 950	290 000	473 950	366 750
Balance	(21 250)	(39 750)	(12 450)	(52 000)	(125 450)	390 750
Opening bal.	0	(21 250)	(61 000)	(73 450)		
Cum. balance	(21 250)	(61 000)	(73 450)	(125 450)		

Exhibit 7.9 Electron: cash budget

Funding working capital

In general, banks and other lending institutions aim to match the term of a loan to the expected useful life of an asset. We will look at finance for capital assets at the end of the next chapter.

If the loan is not to be used for the purchase of fixed assets, then the preferred mechanism is the overdraft facility. Since the amount of working capital required changes frequently, it makes sense to utilise an overdraft to cover this requirement. The banks may seek a personal guarantee and/or a charge over stock. The disadvantage of an overdraft is that it is repayable on demand. Term loans, on the other hand, are repayable over the term of the loan and cannot generally be changed unilaterally.

The size of overdraft required clearly depends on the working capital requirement and has to be agreed at least annually with your bank manager.

You will recall that the current assets less the current liabilities shown on the balance sheet is the business's working capital. But the balance sheet is only a snapshot of the business.

The cash budget, therefore, gives a more accurate figure. Even this, however, is prone to error. Receipts may be delayed by two or three weeks, pushing up the requirement in the middle of a month, though this may not be reflected in month end figures.

Chris runs a small printing business. His business starts in January with average invoiced sales of £5 000 per month, but expects to wait an average of 60 days for payment. He has no credit terms from his suppliers, paying for everything immediately. His cashflow forecast is as shown:

	January	February	March
Receipts			5 000
Expenses			
Materials	1 000	1 000	1 000
Overheads	2 500	2 500	2 500
Drawings	1 000	1 000	1 000
	4 500	4 500	4 500
Balance	(4 500)	(4 500)	500
Cumulative balance	(4 500)	(9 000)	(8 500)

Exhibit 7.10 Overdraft requirements

Customers will generally delay payments to you for as long as possible, though you cannot always do this to your suppliers. As a rule of thumb, it makes sense to aim for minimum working capital

f a month's average sales multiplied by the number of months
ollection period. If you hold large levels of stock and want to be
ather more accurate, then use the following procedure:

)etermine average number of weeks raw material is in stock: e.g.	6
)educt: credit period from suppliers	(4)
,dd: average number of weeks to produce goods or service	2
,dd: average number of weeks finished goods are in stock	2
,dd: average time customers take to pay	8
'otal	14

'he average periods can be calculated as explained in Chapter 4.
' sales for the year are estimated at £500 000 then the maximum
'orking capital required is $14/52 \times 500\,000 = £134\,615$. It would
e more accurate to use the cost of sales (direct and fixed) rather
1an the full selling price.

If the business has no retained earnings, or you have nothing to
ut in, then all the working capital will have to come as an overdraft.
' your business is growing, then your overdraft requirement will
row also. You need to watch for this.

You might choose to speed up payments for your supplies by
1ctoring or invoice discounting. There are a number of factoring
3ents who will take your invoices and give you a proportion of
1e total, around 80 – 90 per cent, immediately. The balance is paid
'hen the customer pays the factor, less their commission which is
ften around 3 – 4 per cent. Factoring is therefore an expensive way
f speeding up cashflow. It does, however, take away all the effort
f chasing up the slow payers. For some businesses, the cost often
quates to a full time person who might otherwise be employed to
1onitor the sales ledger and chase the debtors. Factoring is not
ormally available until you have been in business for three years
nd your turnover is at least £250 000 pa. You should read the
mall print carefully: some factors recharge you for invoices not
·ttled within an agreed period which will give all the cashflow
roblems that factoring is intended to remove.

With invoice discounting, you simply offer a discount in exchange
·r payment within your settlement terms. One difficulty is that
1stomers often take the discount and still pay late. If you intend
> offer a discount arrangement, remember to regard it as a cost

7

of sale and set your price accordingly. If you offer a discount compare it regularly with the cost of having an overdraft. Would it be cheaper to have the overdraft or to offer the discount?

Sensitivity analysis

It is important to know how sensitive your forecast is to changes What happens to your cash position, for example, if sales fall by 5 per cent? What happens if your main supplier increases raw material prices by 12 per cent? Sensitivity analysis is particularly used by financial institutions when considering propositions for a loan. If your business is particularly susceptible to small changes then you probably do not have a sufficiently large profit margin You will thus be less likely to receive the loan required. Of course you may not be able simply to increase prices to improve your margins – that might deter customers. You may find it difficul to cut costs. Are there other ways, however, in which you can push up the margins – increasing output, for example?

Sales change – 20%

	April	May	June	July	Total	Accruals
Sales	0	27 200	61 200	190 400	278 800	605 200
Variable	1 000	43 000	55 160	216 000	315 160	292 600
Fixed	20 000	20 000	20 000	20 000	80 000	
Balance	(21 000)	(35 800)	(13 960)	(45 600)	(116 360)	312 600
Opening bal.	0	(21 000)	(56 800)	(70 760)		
Cum. balance	(21 000)	(56 800)	(70 760)	(116 360)		

Exhibit 7.11 Electron: sensitivity analysis

Look at Exhibit 7.11. A drop of sales of 20 per cent leads to only a small reduction in the overdraft required, but a substantial drop in overall profitability.

Having undertaken your sensitivity analysis, you may need to review elements of your budget.

Formulating the plan: conclusion and checklist

Formulating your plan consists of:

1. Identifying your strategic objectives;
2. Defining operational objectives;
3. Preparing and agreeing a master budget; and
4. Ensuring that everyone with a responsibility for achieving objectives, financial or otherwise, is aware of, and has agreed with, those objectives.

The plan needs to include:

- A sales forecast and sales budget.
- A production budget.
- A materials purchase budget.
- An overheads budget.
- A production cost budget.
- A cash budget.

7

Preparing the sales forecast is the hardest part of producing any plan, especially for a new business. Monitor what happens to sales when you change price. Collect market intelligence by watching your competitors and quizzing your customers.

If a systematic approach is used, the interactions between the various elements will become apparent. Pitfalls will be anticipated which might not otherwise come to light. Remember, you may not get your plan absolutely right first time – you may need several attempts, improving each time, before you produce a workable document.

You need to ensure in the completed budget that:

- All parts are consistent with one another.
- It represents an achievable plan which maximises profit.
- The budgeted profit is adequate to ensure the business's survival and growth.
- All costs are contained and controlled.
- Accounting records are adequate.
- There will be no cashflow problems.

It is important you drive the budgeting and planning process.

There are businesses where budgets have been tried and subsequently failed. This usually happens because the process has not been implemented correctly. Some common pitfalls include:

- Budgets cannot work without an effective business structure. Budgets are not a substitute for organisation.
- Budgets will not solve the problems of poor management.
- Imposed budgets cause frustration and resentment – they are doomed to failure in the long term.
- Care should be taken to ensure that budgets do not become cumbersome, meaningless or expensive.
- The plans should not become too inflexible. The real world changes from day to day. Sometimes events overtake the plan and a new plan becomes necessary.

Exercise

Do you have a cashflow forecast for your business? If not, then put one together for your business for, say, the next six months.

(a) What is your overdraft requirement?
(b) What happens if your sales are 20 per cent lower than forecast?

8 Planning capital assets

Introduction

In the last chapter, we looked at formulating a plan, but that plan was entirely devoted to the trading position of a business. Most businesses require capital assets, albeit of varying levels. This chapter suggests some techniques for costing and financing of capital assets.

Planning fixed assets

Capital assets, or fixed assets, are all those assets which require a capital investment – as opposed to current assets. They have a life of more than one year and generally require substantial expenditure. As with all other aspects of budgeting, you need to think carefully about whether you need a new piece of equipment, a freehold factory, etc, and how you are going to cover its cost.

Fixed assets are acquired for retention and use within the company. Money tied up in fixed assets, therefore, is not available for use in the working capital cycle. From that point of view, as little money as possible should be tied up in fixed assets. However, capital investment can be used to increase sales (by producing more) or reduce operating costs (by automation) so that a trade-off has to be made between the conflicting requirements of the business.

The following points need to be considered before any investment is made:

1. Will the investment produce a return consistent with the risk?
2. Is there sufficient cash to pay for the investment? If additional capital has to be raised, is its cost justified?
3. Has the investment been subjected to a rigorous evaluation – options include:

— consideration of alternatives;
— technical justification;
— consideration of implementation and timing; and
— commercial viability.
4. Have all the consequences of the investment been taken into consideration, for example, increased stock holding?

Equally, however, you do not want to allow all your machinery to become so old and dilapidated that it requires continual expense in repairs and leads to lost sales through being out of commission. New machines may give a better quality of finished product. It makes sense, therefore, to allow for some capital expenditure each year. This is best achieved with an integrated business plan and capital expenditure plan.

Optimum usage

Once fixed assets have been purchased they should be continuously reviewed to ensure that they are still contributing to the business. The following points will need consideration:

1. Each asset should be monitored to ensure it is still producing the required return on investment. This might be achieved by regularly calculating the ratio of sales (or production) to amount invested, or gross profit to amount invested.
2. The expected future contribution from the asset may be below the disposal value in which case the asset should be sold. There may also be a case for replacing an asset with a newer, more efficient asset if the increased return on investment justifies the expenditure.
3. Assets need to be properly maintained to ensure optimum profitability.
4. Productivity may be improved by better production and planning methods.

Depreciation

You will recall from Chapter 3 that depreciation is an annual allowance for wear and tear on equipment. Since fixed assets have a life greater than one year it would clearly be unreasonable to attempt to recover the entire cost from your customers in the year of acquisition. Instead, the cost of the wearing out is spread over the expected life of the asset. This fits with the matching principle also explained in Chapter 3.

Equipment, machinery and vehicles are depreciated, though land is not. Buildings are often also depreciated, especially industrial buildings, though the increase in their value on the open market is frequently greater than the amount that would be depreciated.

To calculate the annual depreciation, you need to estimate the expected life of the asset and be able to estimate any residual or scrap value, although this is often simply regarded as zero. The aim of depreciation is to deduce a fair charge for the use of fixed assets, ensure that this is passed on to your customers and to give a fair profit figure.

There are two main methods for calculating depreciation – straight line and reducing balance.

Straight line depreciation writes off a percentage of the purchase price each year. For example, a vehicle costing £10 000 and depreciated over four years could have 25 per cent (i.e. £2 500) charged to the profit and loss account each year. For most businesses, this is quite sufficient.

Fred has new plant and equipment worth £15 000. He estimates that this will last 7 years and have a scrap value of £1 000. The annual depreciation is, therefore, £2 000. Thus the value of the fixed assets, as shown on the balance sheet, reduces by this amount each year.

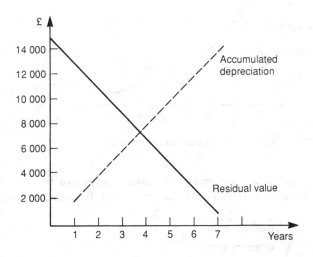

Exhibit 8.1 Straight line depreciation

Reducing balance depreciation is calculated as a percentage of the residual value of the equipment. This might be done, for example, to reflect increasing costs of repairs as the equipment ages. The total cost of depreciation and repairs, however, may remain about constant and the correct total used in calculating how much customers should pay.

Fred decides to use the reducing balance method still writing off his equipment over 7 years. He charges 32% depreciation annually.

Cost	15 000			
Year 1	Depreciation	4 800	Balance	10 200
Year 2		3 264		6 936
Year 3		2 220		4 716
Year 4		1 509		3 207
Year 5		1 026		2 181
Year 6		698		1 483
Year 7		475		1 008

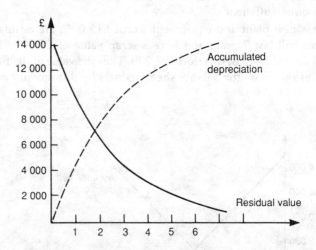

Exhibit 8.2 Reducing balance depreciation

If you know how many years it will take to depreciate fully a piece of equipment, then you can calculate the rate, r, from this equation:

$$r = 100 - \left(\sqrt[n]{\frac{\text{residual value}}{\text{original cost}}} \times 100 \right)$$

where n = estimated life in years

Remember that depreciation does not involve any transfer of money, nor does it build up a reserve of cash to replace equipment. It does, however, reduce the net profit figure which may affect the payment of dividends or the level of ratios.

When prices of equipment are rising, due to inflation, for example, there are good arguments to charge greater amounts of depreciation each year. This is not done under normal accounting conventions however.

Do not confuse depreciation with capital allowances for tax purposes. You may choose any level of depreciation that you think is appropriate. When you submit your accounts to the Inland Revenue, they remove depreciation completely from their calculation of your net profit. They then allow a capital allowance, generally, of 25 per cent on a reducing balance basis. For industrial buildings, there is a 4 per cent allowance on a straight line basis. There is no allowance for commercial buildings.

If you expect your equipment and machines to last at least four years, you may find it helpful to charge 25 per cent depreciation each year also. Your profit calculation will then be similar to the Inland Revenue's calculation. If you also choose the reducing balance basis, then your calculations should be identical. You should note, however, that the Inland Revenue has slightly different rules for depreciation of cars which we will not go into here. If you expect equipment to last less than four years, such as computers, then write them off faster. Remember, the more accurately you reflect depreciation in your budget, the more accurately you will be able to cost your product or service.

If you run a company, company law sets down rules for depreciation of all fixed assets with limited useful lives.

Appraising capital investments

In the early stages of your business it is unlikely that you will need techniques to appraise capital investment. But it is included here for two reasons. First, many suppliers now try to lease equipment to their customers rather than selling it directly. Do you know whether that is cheaper or more expensive than borrowing the money from the bank? Second, and more important, as the business grows you may have opportunities to invest in new projects. Do you know how to appraise which one will give the best return?

Decisions about major investments need to be made carefully, because often large sums of money will be involved and once a decision has been implemented it will be difficult to reverse.

As so often in business, the greatest difficulty will be in estimating the demand for your product, the likely trend and the price people will pay.

You will also have to estimate the useful life of the assets, cost of maintenance, effect (positive or negative) on other aspects of your work, additional working capital required, etc.

When a business makes a capital investment, it does so because it expects to generate income in the future. If this were not the case you would not make the investment. Thus, an investment appraisal compares cash outflows now with the likely cash inflows at some time in the future. Other key variables include the risk that your estimates are incorrect, likely tax allowance changes, inflation, etc. A comprehensive evaluation will be able to allow for all of these.

There are a number of methods often used to appraise investment opportunities. The simplest, and least useful, is to compare total revenue with total expenditure. However, this ignores the cost of the money and ignores any time factor. Other methods include looking at the pay-back and discounted cashflows. The pay-back method looks at how long it takes for the business to recover its initial investment. The most commonly used techniques, however, use discounted cashflow – either to calculate net present value or to calculate the internal rate of return.

Discounting

£100 in your hand now is not the same as £100 receivable in, say, one year because money you have now could be earning interest. If the current rate of interest was 10 per cent, then the money you hold now would be worth £110 in one year. If this were reinvested it would be worth £121 after a further year. This is known as *compounding* and can be formalised thus:

£100 now will be worth:

£100 × (1 + r) in one year

$100 × (1 + r)^2$ in two years

£100 × $(1 + r)^n$ in n years

where r is the current rate of interest

(expressed as a decimal)

So what is the £100 receivable in n years worth now? It is the reverse of the above example:

£100 receivable in one year is worth $\dfrac{100}{(1.1)} = £91$ now

£100 receivable in two years is worth $\dfrac{100}{(1.1)^2} = £83$ now

£100 receivable in n years is worth $\dfrac{100}{(1 + r)^n}$

(where r is the current rate of interest expressed as a decimal)

This procedure is the opposite of compounding and is called *discounting*. In other words, if you were given £83 now and invested it for two years at 10 per cent, it would by then be worth £100.

Discounted cash flow

A *discounted cashflow* (DCF) shows future cashflows, usually over several years, adjusted by a suitable rate, to take account of the timing of the cashflow.

The most reliable method of reviewing specific activities is to calculate the *net present value* (NPV) of each. An activity with a net present value which is positive is worth pursuing; if a choice has to be made, the activity with the highest NPV is the best.

An alternative method is to calculate the *internal rate of return* (IRR). This is the estimated annual percentage profitability on the initial investment, once again allowing for the fact that future receipts are, in effect, worth less than receipts today.

The IRR can be compared to the cost of the capital required. If it is higher, the activity is worth doing; the activity with the highest IRR is the best.

Net present value

The first step in calculating net present value is to estimate the cashflows, both positive and negative, for the expected life of the machine. These then need to be discounted to present values at a predetermined rate of interest. This is often taken as the cost of capital to your business, particularly appropriate if you will need to borrow the money from the bank. If you have the money already available, then use the opportunity cost, i.e. the rate of return you can achieve with the money on deposit.

If you have a computer or calculator, the discount factors can easily be calculated using the formula shown above, otherwise tables of discount factors are available to save you having to do the calculations.

Let us look at an example. Charlton runs a chocolate factory and wonders whether to install a new chocolate line at a cost of £25 000. The machine will last four years. He has estimated the net cashflows as shown in Exhibit 8.3. The net cashflow is the net profit, though you should ignore interest and tax. This raises the problem, again, of how to spread the fixed cost across several products. However, that is clearly essential if you are going to achieve a reasonably accurate answer.

Year	Cashflow	Discount factor	Present value	Rate 0.13
0	− 25 000	1.00	− 25 000	
1	6 000	0.88	5 310	
2	9 000	0.78	7 048	
3	12 000	0.69	8 317	
4	15 000	0.61	9 200	
NPV			4 874	

Exhibit 8.3 Charlton's Chocolates

The present value outflows are deducted from the inflows to arrive at the net present value. If the NPV is negative, then the project should be rejected. Charlton starts with a 13 per cent interest rate. This is the best return he could achieve from his bank at present. The NPV is £4 874 so Charlton should proceed (unless there is a different project possible with a higher NPV). If interest rates can be expected to change over the four years, the conclusions will be affected.

Year	Cashflow	Discount factor	Present value	Rate 0.21
0	− 25 000	1.00	− 25 000	
1	6 000	0.83	4 959	
2	9 000	0.68	6 147	
3	12 000	0.56	6 774	
4	15 000	0.47	6 998	
NPV			− 123	

Exhibit 8.4 Charlton's Chocolates

If Charlton has to borrow the money he has been told that he will have to pay 21 per cent APR. This gives an NPV of − 123 in which case the project should be rejected. A positive NPV means that a surplus will be made, allowing for the interest payments. A negative NPV means that there would be a loss.

Let us now compare the cost of leasing with the cost of purchase of a photocopier costing £12 000. If you buy, you have an immediate outflow of £12 000. If you lease, you have quarterly payments of £755 for five years. Which is preferable? Rather than calculating all the figures on a quarterly basis, we will take the amount paid by the mid-point of each year.

Year	Cashflow	Discount factor	Present value	Rate 0.14
0	1 510	1.00	1 510	
1	3 020	0.88	2 649	Amount
2	3 020	0.77	2 324	755
3	3 020	0.67	2 038	
4	3 020	0.59	1 788	
5	1 510	0.52	784	
NPV			11 094	

Exhibit 8.5   Photocopier lease

If you pay cash, the total cost will be £12 000. If the opportunity cost of that money is 14 per cent, then the total NPV of leasing is £11 094 − so lease!

Do not confuse the investment decision with the decision of whether to buy or lease. The decision whether to proceed with a project needs to be made first. Once you are certain that you wish to proceed, then you are ready to decide whether to buy or lease.

Let us look at one last example. You are wondering whether to buy or lease a new car. If you lease, you will have to make an immediate payment of £2 400 with two further payments in the following two years. The opportunity cost is once again 14 per cent.

Year	Cashflow	Discount factor	Present value	Rate 0.14
0	2 400	1.00	2 400	
1	2 400	0.88	2 105	Amount
2	2 400	0.77	1 874	2 400
NPV			6 352	

Exhibit 8.6   Car lease

This gives an NPV of £6 352. If you can buy the car for less money than this, buy it; otherwise, lease it. Remember that if you have to borrow the money, you must make the calculations with the interest rate which you will have to pay.

All these NPV calculations have assumed that interest rates stay constant for the period of the lease. A combination of inflation and a reducing interest rate may tip the scales in favour of buying.

So far, we have ignored the effects of tax and inflation on the DCF calculation. Unless you are good at seeing into the future, both are difficult to account for. Let us apply current tax rates and tax allowances to the example of Charlton's Chocolates.

Year	Cashflow	Tax allowance	Tax	Net cashflow	Discount factor	Present value
0	− 25 000			− 25 000	1.00	− 25 000
1	6 000	6 250		12 250	0.83	10 124
2	9 000	4 688	− 1 500	12 188	0.68	8 324
3	12 000	3 516	− 2 250	13 266	0.56	7 488
4	15 000	2 637	− 3 000	14 637	0.47	6 828
5		1 978	− 3 750	− 1 772	0.39	− 683
NPV						7 081

Exhibit 8.7 Effect of taxation

The capital equipment attracts a capital allowance of 25 per cent each year on a reducing balance basis, though the effect of this does not work through until the year after the purchase. The extra profit is taxed (for a small company) at 25 per cent, again, in the year after the profit arises. For many projects, the tax effect may be insignificant, but for those where the decision is marginal, it becomes more important.

The effect of inflation is harder to account for. Imagine that your business has made a return of 15 per cent on capital and that the rate of inflation is 10 per cent – what is the real rate of return?

$$\text{Real rate of return} = \frac{1 + \text{nominal rate of return}}{1 + \text{rate of inflation}} - 1$$

Write the rates as decimals rather than as percentages. In our example, therefore, the real rate of return = 1.15/1.1 − 1 = 0.045 or nearly 5 per cent, as you would guess intuitively.

Rather than trying to allow for the effects of inflation by increasing your cashflows, it makes sense to use figures which represent current purchasing power.

Internal rate of return

To calculate the internal rate of return, you will need to calculate a number of NPVs at different discount rates until an NPV of zero is achieved. This can usually be done graphically by choosing low and high discount rates, or else can be done quite easily on a computerised spreadsheet. The discount rate when NPV is equal to zero, is the yield or return on investment for the project.

Year	Cashflow	Discount factor	Present value	Rate 0.20774
	− 25 000	1.00	− 25 000	
	6 000	0.83	4 968	
	9 000	0.69	6 170	
	12 000	0.57	6 812	
	15 000	0.47	7 050	
NPV			0	

Exhibit 8.8 Internal rate of return

Exhibit 8.8 shows Charlton's Chocolates cashflows again. This time, however, the rate has been adjusted until the NPV is zero. As you can see, the yield is 20.8 per cent. If this yield is greater than the cost of borrowing the money, or greater than your predetermined yield, then undertake the project. As can be seen, there is little difference between the methods of calculation. This technique is normally used by larger companies, who need to know the precise yield, and who have a minimum cut-off, below which they will not accept projects.

If you have a computer available it is easy to calculate the internal rate of return by successively trying new values until you achieve an NPV of zero. Otherwise, you calculate the NPV using two rates of return. The rate of return to give an NPV of zero can then be calculated by interpolation or by drawing a graph.

Replacement of equipment

The appraisal techniques shown so far are appropriate for taking decisions regarding the undertaking of a new project or to assess the best method or obtaining equipment. They cannot be used to compare the use of existing equipment with the replacement by new equipment. In this case, simply look up to one year ahead. Is the cost of using the existing equipment (running costs, repairs, depreciation, etc) less than the cost of new equipment (depreciation, running costs, debt/lease costs, etc)? Is the quality provided by the existing equipment satisfactory? If the answer to both these questions is yes, then continue using the existing equipment. Review your decision again in one year's time.

Once you have decided to replace the equipment, you can then use DCF to decide whether to buy or lease.

To determine the internal rate of return, pick two rates thought to be close to the likely rate of return. Calculate the NPV. Plot the results on a graph. (A rate of 19% gives a NPV of 999; a rate of 23% gives an NPV of −1171.)

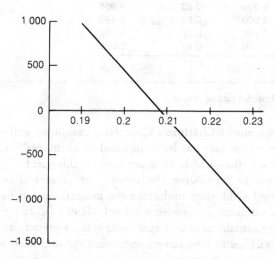

Exhibit 8.9 Graphical interpolation

The actual rate of return can then be read from the graph as about .207.

Funding capital assets

Equity, or shareholder capital, is the money introduced into a business by the proprietor(s) and anyone else willing to invest capital in the hope of getting future returns. If it is a company, then the equity is introduced in exchange for shares. If the business does well, the directors declare a dividend each year. If it does very well, may be floated on the USM or stock market, in which case the original shareholdings will become valuable. Often, though, shareholders' capital is locked into small businesses. Advance corporation tax is deductible from dividend payments. Even if dividend payments are not paid, corporation tax is still payable on all profits.

Loan capital, or debt, is money lent to a business. Normally, the period of the loan is determined according to the life of the asset for which it is used. A long-term loan for premises; a medium- or short-term loan for equipment; and an overdraft for working capital. Term loans are preferable to overdrafts since overdrafts are repayable on demand; however, it is unlikely that a term loan will be available for working capital. Interest on loans is tax deductible, whereas dividends are paid out of profit.

The purchase of buildings or land can probably be spread over 20 or 25 years with the asset used as security for the loan. It is unusual, however, for the banks to provide the entire sum required, preferring to limit their loan to 75 per cent of the value of the assets.

Once you have built up a track record with your bank, you should be able to attract medium term loans, say three to seven years, to cover the cost of plant and equipment. The term of the loan will be dependent not only on the amount borrowed but also on the expected life of the equipment. Computers, for example, which rapidly become obsolete and increasingly expensive to repair, are unlikely to attract a loan of more than two or three years. Shop fittings, or office equipment, on the other hand, are likely to last a long time and need little maintenance, so you would be more easily able to obtain a loan over a longer period.

Sometimes long-term debt can be introduced as a debenture which normally receives a fixed rate of interest and is repayable in full at the end of the term. Debentures sometimes carry options to turn them into shares. Long-term debt is usually included with the capital in the balance sheet, whereas short-term debt, and especially overdrafts, are treated as current liabilities.

Most banks look for a gearing of about 1 to 1. The gearing is the proportion of debt to total finance; the higher the gearing, the more debt there is relative to equity. Once your business starts to grow, therefore, it will be essential to introduce more money as equity or else retain substantial profits in the business.

It is often possible for businesses to buy equipment on hire purchase, leasing or lease purchasing. These have often been treated as 'off balance sheet' forms of finance, though it is now normal practice to show the outstanding payments as current or longer-term

8

liabilities. Lease companies will not have the same concerns about gearing as the banks. They will, however, be interested in your cashflow and whether you can afford the repayments. Unlike when buying the equipment with your own money or with a bank loan, the equipment will remain the property of the leasing company. The lessee has the legal right to use the equipment for the period of the lease assuming, of course, that the lease payments are up to date. At the end of the lease, the equipment reverts to the lessor, although it is often possible to buy the equipment for a small sum.

Planning capital assets: conclusion and checklist

It is just as important to plan for the acquisition of capital assets as it is to budget for all other aspects of the business. You need to consider carefully before investing large sums of money in new equipment, however.

- Is your existing equipment satisfactory?
- If you have decided to replace equipment, will you lease or buy
- Is a new product worth pursuing — will it give you a suitable rate of return? Would your money give a better return if invested elsewhere?

Exercise

You run a mechanical engineering machine shop undertaking sub-contract work. You have £20 000 available to buy a new machine but cannot decide between a milling machine at £18 000 or a lathe at £17 500. You cannot afford both. You anticipate that the net cash flow for the next four years for the lathe will be £9 000 pa after which the lathe will be redundant. The milling machine will only generate £7 000 net pa but it will last for six years. You could achieve 14% long term if you simply invested the money. Do you buy a machine and, if so, which one?

9 Book-keeping requirements

Introduction □ Accounting records □ Collecting the information □ The VAT return □ Conclusion and checklist

Introduction

This chapter is intended as a reminder of the principles of book-keeping and covers the key records. Those readers wishing to read more about book-keeping should refer to *Book-keeping and Accounting* by Geoffrey Whitehead available in this series.

In the early stages of running a business, the most cost-effective method of book-keeping is to keep the books manually. A good book-keeping system will provide you with all the information regularly to compare your business's performance with your plan. In due course, you may computerise or buy in a book-keeper, but it will still be helpful to understand how the book-keeping works.

It is important for all businesses to exercise daily cash control – all cheques and cash should be paid into the bank on the day they are received. Any cash in hand, in excess of short-term requirements, should be placed in an interest-bearing account.

Accounting records

Many people insist on the desirability of double entry book-keeping, in which every transaction is recorded twice – as a debit and as a credit – in different accounts. For many businesses this may well be extremely helpful. It has the added advantage that trial balances can quickly be determined by summarising the balance from each account, and also that it forms the basis of all computerised book-keeping systems. Since the system is self-balancing (i.e. debits always equal credits) the search for errors is made easier.

Many businesses, however, prefer to use simpler book-keeping systems. Since the purpose of this book is to look at financial control,

9

not book-keeping, we will look at a simple single entry book-keeping system based on the use of cash analysis books. There are a number of proprietary cash book systems available (e.g. Simplex, Finco, Kalamazoo, etc). There are all designed to simplify the book-keeping process as much as possible. However, it is still important to understand the principles of book-keeping.

To keep adequate records, you need four separate books: the cash book; the sales ledger; the purchase ledger; and a wages book. Of these, the cash book is the one that keeps track of all payments and receipts by the business and is absolutely essential. In addition, you may find it helpful to keep a petty cash book and a stock book.

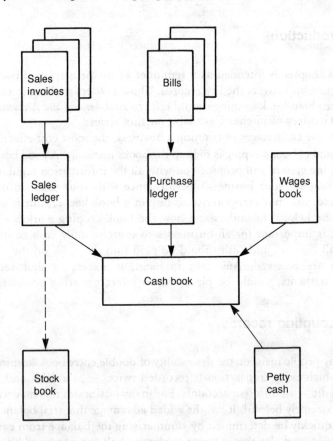

Exhibit 9.1

Cash book

Look at Exhibit 9.2 which shows a typical cash book layout. An analysis cash book should be used which has a number of columns across the page. The number and headings of the columns will depend on the categories of receipts and payments which are likely to be incurred regularly. It is conventional for receipts to be recorded on the left-hand page and payments on the right-hand page, and for one line to be regarded as going across the double page spread with one entry per line.

Every time a cheque is received or issued, the total amount should be entered in the column headed 'bank' on the relevant page and then analysed into the appropriate columns. This immediate analysis is to enable you to monitor the major and the most important items. On the payments side, you would certainly expect to include raw materials, wages, premises costs and drawings. You would probably choose other headings depending on the likely areas of expenditure by your business. Payments made by standing order or direct debit should also be recorded. Note in the example, the payment for wages which has not been by cheque, but by Autopay. At the end of the month all the columns should be totalled. The sum of the separate totals should equal the addition of the total (i.e. the bank) column. At the end of each month deduct the expenditure (£15 940) from the income (£13 708) to give the net cashflow for the month. Then add the figure carried forward from the previous month to give the carry down figure (£361). As you would expect, this is also the balance that should be in the bank. If the figure is negative – i.e. you have an overdraft – you should carry it forward on to the expenditure page.

The cash book should exactly represent every movement on the bank account. At the end of each month, you should reconcile the cash book with your bank statement. This is a means of ensuring that the cash book and statements do agree.

Look at the statement in Exhibit 9.3. If there are additional items, such as bank charges, interest, standing orders, etc, then these should be recorded in the cash book.

As you can see, all the transactions in the cash book have been recorded except two that occurred too late in the month. These are the cheque issued to MSL and the cheque received from Frondbury Hall.

You should reconcile the figures by taking the bank balance you have calculated from your records, deducting uncleared receipts and adding back uncleared payments. This should give the statement

Receipts

Date	Name	Ref no	Bank	Sales	Other	VAT
1/6	Carried forward		2 593.00			
15/6	J Giles	9015	2 300.00	2 000.00		300.00
20/6	H Jones Ltd	9011	862.50	750.00		112.50
21/6	B Smith	9012	1 322.50	1 150.00		172.50
21/6	Electron Ltd	9014	1 886.00	1 640.00		246.00
25/6	Hunters	9019	1 989.50	1 730.00		259.50
25/6	Robinson Electrical	9018	2 472.50	2 150.00		322.50
29/6	Frondbury Hall	9020	2 875.00	2 500.00		375.00
			13 708.00	11 920.00	0.00	1 788.00
Monthly balance			(2 232.00)			
Bank balance			361.00			

Payments

Date	Details	Chq no	Bank	VAT	Materials	Marketing	Travel	Premises	Capital	Wages Tax/NI	Petty cash	Other
1/6	Andy's Autos	813	1 900.00						1 900.00			
10/6	City Council	814	1 000.00					1 000.00				
10/6	Shell Garages	815	115.00	15.00			100.00					
17/6	Inland Revenue	816	2 100.00							2 100.00		
25/6	Borthwick	817	3 450.00	450.00	3 000.00							
25/6	Wages	a/p	5 000.00							5 000.00		
25/6	Petty cash	818	75.00								75.00	
28/6	MSL	819	2 300.00	300.00		2 000.00						
			15 940.00	765.00	3 000.00	2 000.00	100.00	1 000.00	1 900.00	7 100.00	75.00	0.00

Exhibit 9.2 Cash book

National Westminster Bank PLC				CONFIDENTIAL
ANYTOWN BRANCH	Account	CURRENT		SHEET NO. 21
Telephone 091 999999	Statement date	8 JUL 1990	Account no.	12345678

Date	Details	Withdrawals	Deposits	Balance (£)	
3 JUN	Balance from Sheet no. 20			2,593.00	
4 JUN	000813	1,900.00		693.00	
15 JUN	000815	115.00			
15 JUN	000814	1,000.00		422.00	OD
15 JUN	100034 CC		2,300.00	1,878.00	
19 JUN	000816	2,100.00		222.00	OD
21 JUN	100035		4,071.00	3,849.00	
25 JUN	AUTOPAY SERVICE	5,000.00		1,151.00	OD
25 JUN	100036		1,989.50	838.50	
25 JUN	ROBINSON ELEC		2,472.50	3,311.00	
27 JUN	000817	3,450.00		139.00	OD
27 JUN	000818	75.00		214.00	OD
8 JUL	Balance to Sheet no. 22				

Key SO Standing Order   DV Dividend   CC Cash &/or Cheques   Auto   AC Automated Cash   PY Payroll   Interest - see over
EC Eurocheque   TR Transfer   CP Card Purchase   withdrawals   DD Direct Debit   OD Overdrawn

Exhibit 9.3 Bank statement

balance. If it does not, then you have an error somewhere.

Note that the cash book is showing a positive balance, but that there is actually an overdraft at the bank. It is important to watch the timing of payments in order not to become more overdrawn than you would like. Even if your cashflow forecast shows a positive balance at the end of every month, there may be occasions during the month when this problem might arise.

Bank reconciliation	
Bank balance	361.00
less: uncleared receipts	2 875.00
plus: uncleared payments	2 300.00
Statement balance	(214.00)

Exhibit 9.4 Bank reconciliation

The sales ledger

The sales ledger records the amount of sales for the month, the amount of cash received and what is due to the business at the end of the month. Every time an invoice is issued it should be recorded in the sales ledger. A copy of the invoice should be retained, showing the details of the work for which the invoice has been issued, a unique invoice number, the VAT rate and the amount of VAT.

A typical format for a sales ledger is shown in Exhibit 9.5. As can be seen, there is a column to enter the date when an invoice is paid. It is thus extremely easy to see which invoices are outstanding so as to chase them. You may also find it helpful to add up the outstanding debtors at the end of each month and make a note of the figure. Compare the invoices paid in June with the cash book in Exhibit 9.2.

Invoice date	Customer	Invoice number	Net amount	VAT	Total	Date paid
1/5	H Jones Ltd	9 011	750.00	112.50	862.50	20/6
3/5	B Smith Ltd	9 012	1 150.00	172.50	1 322.50	21/6
5/5	Hunters	9 013	2 150.00	322.50	2 472.50	
5/5	Electron Ltd	9 014	1 640.00	246.00	1 886.00	21/6
5/5	J Giles	9 015	2 000.00	300.00	2 300.00	15/6
25/5	Mulholland Ltd	9 016	7 500.00	1 125.00	8 625.00	
26/5	Electron Ltd	9 017	6 000.00	900.00	6 900.00	
26/5	Robinson Electrical	9 018	2 150.00	322.50	2 472.50	25/6
27/5	Hunters	9 019	1 730.00	259.50	1 989.50	25/6
27/5	Frondbury Hall	9 020	2 500.00	375.00	2 875.00	29/6
			27 570.00	4 135.50	31 705.50	
				Debtors	17 997.50	

Exhibit 9.5 Sales ledger

This format will also satisfy the requirements for accounting for VAT (see later).

The purchase ledger

Many people are more cavalier with bills, often tossing them in a desk drawer until the end of the month. Whilst this is simple, it is bad practice. You do not know how much you owe to your suppliers or even whether you still have all the bills – some are sure to get mislaid resulting in unpaid and, therefore, upset suppliers.

The purchase ledger works in a similar manner to the sales ledger and is used to record all suppliers' invoices and to show those which are still unpaid (and allow VAT to be accounted for). A similar format to the payments side of the cash book is generally used, though it excludes columns, such as wages, for which you do not receive bills. Once again, you may find it helpful to add up the outstanding creditors at the end of each month and make a note of the figure.

Date recd	Supplier	Ref no	Total	VAT	Mtls	Mktg	Travel	Prem-ises	Capi-tal	Date paid
3/5	Andy's Autos	951	1 900						1 900	1/6
3/5	City Council Rates	952	1 000					1 000		10/6
5/5	Borthwick	953	3 450	450	3 000					25/6
5/5	ComputerSynch Ltd	954	2 300	300					2 000	
6/5	Rent A Shed	955	2 900					2 900		
7/5	Shell Garages	956	115	15			100			10/6
10/5	MSL	957	2 300	300	2 000					28/6
21/5	Borthwick	958	2 070	270	1 800					
			16 035	1 335	4 800	2 000	100	3 900	3 900	
	Creditors		7 250							

Figure 9.6 Purchase ledger

As with the sales ledger, the VAT figures can be quickly extracted when required.

Whilst it is not essential to use purchase order numbers, it makes good sense. If you use a purchase ledger, you will be able to number the bills as they are received and record the number in the ledger so that you can easily retrieve the bill if a query arises later.

If you are placing orders for goods to be received at some date in the future, then you should give an order number. If you are likely to have a lot of goods on order at any time, then set up an order book so that you can quickly see the level of your commitment. Allocate unique numbers and use order forms. If you do not place many orders then you may think this is undesirably bureaucratic. Do not be like one business, known to the author, who made up order numbers by reversing the six digits of the date and adding four extra digits chosen at random.

The wages book

When you start to employ people, you should inform the Inland Revenue who will provide a very comprehensive pack with forms for recording payments and deductions for each employee and instructions on their use. It is not essential to have a wages book in addition since it only records the same information. However, the payments and deductions for all employees for each week or month will be summarised together if you do use one.

Wages books are designed for recording wages and deductions and show the break down of the total wages paid by a business in any week or month. They record the following details for each employee:

- Gross pay.
- Employee's National Insurance contributions.
- Pension and/or other deductions.
- Net pay.
- Employer's National Insurance contributions.

The wages book will not be described any further here. The net wage payments and the payments of tax and NI must be transferred to the cash book when the cheques are issued. Note that these are not payments that would be recorded in the purchase ledger since they are not purchases. Once you start to employ several staff you might find it helpful to use one of the special schemes operated by the banks such as Autopay. With Autopay you simply send one form to the bank with all the net payments listed. The bank then automatically credits your employees' accounts on the day you say and debits your account accordingly.

The petty cash book

Most businesses will require to have some cash available, for example, to buy stamps, coffee, etc. Cash kept on the premises should, of course, be locked away. Payments in cash also need to be recorded. The petty cash book will show all cash receipts and payments in a similar format to the cash book although the detailed analysis may not be necessary. Amounts shown as received in the petty cash book should match the amounts in the petty cash column on the payments page of the cash book, i.e. when a cheque is cashed. The amount of cash in the petty cash box at any time should equal the balance shown by the petty cash book.

Accounting records for cash businesses

Some businesses – for example, retail – deal almost entirely in cash on the sale of their goods rather than invoicing and awaiting payment at a later date. Clearly, they can simplify their accounting procedures.

A retail business would total up the entire amount of cash taken, say, each day. This would be paid into the bank and simply shown on the receipts side of the cash book as 'Tuesday's takings', for example.

Many businesses which receive large amounts of money as cash also tend, however, to use some of that cash to pay bills (and reduce their bank charges). Clearly, you cannot simply take money out of the till without recording it. These payments also need to be recorded in the main cash book. One possibility is to have two books, one which covers all cheque transactions and one which covers all cash transactions (though this is obviously more important than the petty cash book described above). When cash is paid into the bank, or when a cheque is cashed to provide money, say, for the float, then an entry has to be made in both books. An alternative, however, is to add a 'cash' column after the 'bank' column in the cash analysis book. Receipts and payments are then shown either in the bank column or in the cash column – but not both. They are then analysed into the appropriate columns. Transfers between bank and cash are thus shown on both pages, but otherwise the book is kept exactly as described above.

Look at the example in Exhibit 9.7. All receipts come in as cash. Each time the cash register is reconciled, the total is transferred to the cash book, normally at the end of each day. Payments are sometimes made by cheque and sometimes by cash. When surplus cash is transferred to the bank it is shown as a debit in the cash column (i.e. on the right-hand page) and as a credit in the bank column (i.e. on the left-hand page).

This can be quickly checked by adding the opening figures to give £3 093, adding the total in, whether bank or cash (£12 900), deducting the total cost out, whether bank or cash (£11 685) which gives a closing balance of £4 308. This is also the answer if you simply add the bank and cash closing balances.

When you have only a bank column, the total received will eventually equal the total income to the business – when all the debts are paid – and it is the same for the expenditure. If you have a bank column and a cash column, however, do not make the mistake of adding the two together to tell you your income or expenditure. Because of the transfers, they simply show cash moving around the system. You need to use the appropriate analysis columns instead.

Receipts

Date	Name	Ref no	Bank	Cash	Sales	VAT
1/6	Carried forward		2 593.00	500.00		
15/6	Sales			2 300.00	2 000.00	300.00
15/6	Transfer from cash		2 000.00			
20/6	Sales			2 300.00	2 000.00	300.00
20/6	Transfer from cash		2 000.00			
25/6	Sales			2 300.00	2 000.00	300.00
25/6	Transfer from cash		2 000.00			
			6 000.00	6 900.00	6 000.00	900.00
	Monthly balance		1 455.00	(240.00)		
	Balances		4 048.00	260.00		

Payments

Date	Details	Chq no	Bank	Cash	VAT	Materials	Marketing	Travel	Premises	Capital	Wages Tax/NI	Other
1/6	Valentines	429	1 150.00		150.00	1 000.00						
10/6	City Council	430	1 000.00						1 000.00			
10/6	Shell Garages			115.00	15.00			100.00				
15/6	Transfer to bank			2 000.00								
17/6	G Fraser			575.00	75.00	500.00						
20/6	Transfer to bank			2 000.00								
25/6	Boris Ltd	431	1 150.00		150.00	1 000.00						
25/6	Wages		900.00								900.00	
25/6	Transfer to bank			2 000.00								
27/6	Drawings			450.00								450.00
28/6	MSL	432	345.00		45.00		300.00					
			4 545.00	7 140.00	435.00	2 500.00	300.00	100.00	1 000.00	0.00	900.00	450.00

Exhibit 9.7 Cash book

Stock control

If you do not carry much stock, you may wish to skip this section. If, however, you have large amounts of working capital tied up in stock, then you should have a book to monitor your stock position, as raw materials are bought and consumed, as work in progress continues through the factory, and as finished goods are sold. Some businesses, such as retailers, buy in finished goods, but they still need to control stock carefully.

Stock is normally valued at cost or net realisable value, whichever is the lower. Net realisable value is the amount of money you might receive if you were forced to sell quickly. It is reasonable to assume raw materials (e.g. wood, flour, electronic components) could be resold for the sum at which they were bought. But half-completed work in progress may only have scrap value. If you are trading, you may get caught out by changes in price or new models being introduced by the manufacturer, recently prevalent in computing for example.

		Materials received	Issued to production	Stock remaining
	Opening balance			3 000
5/5	Borthwick	3 000		6 000
6/5			2 000	4 000
13/5			2 000	2 000
20/5			2 000	0
21/5	Borthwick	1 800		1 800
27/5			1 600	200
	Total	4 800	7 600	200

Exhibit 9.8 Stock record: raw materials

As raw materials are received, they are recorded. As raw materials are issued to production, they are also recorded. For the sake of simplicity, we will value work in progress and finished goods only as the cost of materials.

When goods are finished, they cease to be work in progress and become finished goods stock. As they are dispatched, they are deducted from the total finished goods stock.

Compare the values of stock dispatched with the sales ledger. You will see that the sales price is four times the raw material cost. This means the gross margin for this business is 75 per cent. If you record stock in this way, it will be very straightforward to find the total

		Materials received	Goods finished	WIP remaining
	Opening balance			2 000
6/5		2 000		4 000
6/5			1 900	2 100
13/5		2 000		4 100
13/5			1 800	2 300
20/5		2 000		4 300
20/5			2 200	2 100
27/5		1 600		3 700
27/5			1 800	1 900
	Total	7 600	7 700	1 900

Exhibit 9.9 Stock record: work in progress

value of stock remaining (for inclusion on the balance sheet) and the total cost of goods sold (for inclusion on the profit and loss account).

If you have a service business, or only use low levels of raw materials, then you can dispense with the stock control records. If raw material stock is used in more than one product then you need to allocate the cost of those materials when they are released to manufacture. By the time that you have grown that large, you will probably have introduced a computerised book-keeping system with

		Goods received	Goods dispatched	Goods remaining
	Opening balance			2 000
1/5	H Jones Ltd		187	1 813
3/5	B Smith Ltd		287	1 526
5/5	Hunters		537	989
5/5	Electron Ltd		410	579
5/5	J Giles		500	79
6/5		1 900		1 979
13/5		1 800		3 779
20/5		2 200		5 979
25/5	Mulholland Ltd		1 875	4 104
26/5	Electron Ltd		1 500	2 604
26/5	Robinson Electrical		537	2 067
27/5		1 800		3 867
27/5	Hunters		432	3 435
27/5	Frondbury Hall		625	2 810
	Total	7 700	6 890	2 810

Exhibit 9.10 Stock record: finished goods

a stock control facility. If you are retailing, you will probably just record everything together since otherwise the records would become too unwieldy, and without a clever till it would be impossible to record invididual items as they are sold.

Collecting the information

As will be apparent from the above, there is nothing particularly complicated about recording all the data relating to sales and purchases, to receipts and payments.

If you produce more than one product or service, however, you will want to be able to attribute sales and purchases to the appropriate product.

For the overhead costs, there is little choice but to add them altogether and to spread them between products as described in Chapter 6. The direct costs, however, do need to be attributed in some way. If you only have a small choice of products then one simple way to do this is to have a separate column for each product or service both in the sales ledger and in the purchase ledger. Remember it is the sales and purchases figures that are appropriate, not the receipts and expenses. These figures can be recorded in the cash book as described earlier with no need to distinguish them.

Sources of funds		Application of funds	
Current liabilities		Current assets	
Creditors	7 270	Cash at bank	361
Loans		Debtors	17 998
VAT	2 801	Raw material stock	200
		Work in progress	1 900
		Finished goods	2 810
Total	10 071		
Capital & Reserves			
P&L	5 695		
Reserves	7 503		
	23 269	Total	23 269
Revenue		Expenses	
Sales	27 570	Purchases	14 700
		Other	7 175
	21 875		21 875
Net profit	5 695		

Exhibit 9.11 Financial summary

If you have several products and this method is impractical, you may choose to have a separate sales ledger and a separate purchases ledger for each product. You will then need to have an additional purchases ledger for those overheads not directly attributable to a particular product.

You may find it helpful in the cash book to distinguish between those items which are recorded in the purchases ledgers and those which are not (such as salaries). In this way, it is possible at any time to derive an accurate financial position showing income, debtors, expenditure and creditors.

You could choose to introduce a system of cost codes. However, this involves additional work each month calculating the income and expenditure according to the codes. Splitting the sales and purchases ledger effectively gives codes anyway. When you computerise your book-keeping, you can then give cost codes to the different items and allow the computer to carry out the calculations.

The VAT return

If your turnover is below £250 000 you may account for output VAT on an invoice basis (i.e. what you have invoiced) or on a cash basis (i.e. what you have actually received). You must, however, have the agreement of Customs and Excise before you use the cash

Month	Output tax	Input tax
April	3 750	1 500
May	4 136	1 335
June	3 900	1 350
Totals	11 786	4 185
Due	7 601	

Month	Invoice income	Expenses
April	25 000	17 000
May	27 570	19 700
June	26 000	16 000
Totals	78 570	52 700

Exhibit 9.12 VAT summary

accounting scheme. If your turnover is over £250 000 you must account for output VAT on an invoice basis. You may account for input VAT on a purchases basis (i.e. whether or not you have paid for goods) or on a cash basis.

Whichever method you choose, the figures are quickly available from the sales and purchase ledgers or from the cash books if you follow the simple suggestions made earlier.

These can be summarised as shown in Exhibit 9.12 and the relevant figures can then be easily transferred to the quarterly VAT return. Remember that the expenditure includes some payments that are zero rated or exempt from VAT, but the expenditure total should exclude VAT, wages, tax, loan repayments, etc.

There are a number of specific rules for some activities, such as the construction industry. Retailers normally operate a retail scheme to take care of the fact that some goods may be standard rated and some zero rated. If you are in any doubt, then contact your nearest VAT office.

Book-keeping requirements: conclusion and checklist

Accounting records, if properly maintained, can be used on a day-to-day basis to see how a business is doing. At least monthly, there are a number of tasks which must be done carefully.

Ensure you bring the cash book up to date and carry out a bank reconciliation. The cash book may need to be updated for any omitted entries such as standing orders or bank charges. The cash book balance represents the business's liquidity – it is the cash immediately available to the business.

Reconciliation should be done at the end of every month. The balance in the cash book is likely to differ from the balance on the bank statement due to time-lags but the difference should be reconciled as shown earlier.

Compare the actual cashflow figures with the budgeted figures. That is why many cashflow forecast forms have columns for both forecast and actual.

You should have set up a book-keeping system which includes the following:

- Cash book.
- Sales ledger.
- Purchase ledger.

- Wages book.
- Petty cash book.
- Stock control book (if appropriate).

The system should be able to give the following information simply and easily at any time:

- Cash position.
- Outstanding debtors.
- Outstanding creditors.
- Stock.

10 Analysis of variances

Introduction □ What is variance analysis? □ Sales variances □ Material and labour variances □ Overheads variances □ The operating statement □ The cashflow statement □ Aged debtors □ Aged creditors □ Stock □ The balance sheet □ Contribution by product line □ Capital expenditure report □ Labour turnover report □ Management information systems □ Review the figures with your staff □ Conclusion and checklist □ Exercise

Introduction

The most important part of exercising control is analysing the figures and comparing them both historically and against the plan. By the end of this chapter, you will be able to assess the key figures that you need to monitor for decision making in your business and will have been introduced to appropriate analysis techniques.

What is variance analysis?

A variance is simply the difference between your budgeted and your actual performance. Whether it is positive or negative, it will have consequences for the overall running of the business, and action must be taken to allow for it.

As was explained earlier, the costing and pricing system for your business is based on estimating future costs. There is a clear need, therefore, to monitor actual costs against budgeted costs to ensure that you are not going off track. You should monitor volumes as well as values.

If you are using standard times and standard costs to calculate the direct cost of your products, it is even more important to monitor the variances.

If you record all the data suggested in the last chapter, then you should be able to carry out all the basic variance analysis. Some variances, such as labour turnover, can be reviewed less frequently. Many businesses fail because action has not been taken to rectify problems that variance analysis would have highlighted. Use the data that you have recorded.

Review the variances regularly, and at least once per month, after you have balanced the books. If you discover a variance, then ask what caused it. Watch for variances simply caused by differences in timing – have orders been brought forward or delayed? How accurate are your budgeted figures? If sales are below budget, was the budget over-optimistic? Can the business survive on lower levels of sales? Can you compensate by an increase on price? Or will a price decrease generate more sales? Are you spending too much on raw materials? Can you find cheaper suppliers? Can your business become more efficient? Remember, to be effective, analysing variances has to consider more than just differences in cash. Indeed, there may be major variances even though the overall cash position remains more or less constant.

The following figures should be reviewed regularly:

- Sales, enquiry and order position.
- Material and labour usage.
- Overheads.
- Monthly trading reports.
- Cash position/cash forecast.
- Aged debtors report.
- Aged creditors report.
- Stock.
- Balance sheet and ratios.
- Capital expenditure.
- Staff turnover.

The next few paragraphs are designed to help you keep track of variances and ratios within your own business. We will follow the progress of William's Widgets. He is half-way through the year, with costs slightly up and sales revenue slightly down. He normally gives customers, and expects from suppliers, 30 days' credit, although this does not always occur.

Sales variances

As you might guess, you should monitor sales for each product both by volume and by value. A sales revenue comprises a sales price variance and a sales volume variance. If your price drops but your volume increases this may give an apparently favourable sales

variance, whereas your costs as a proportion of the sales price may
have risen significantly. Look at Exhibit 10.1.

Volume	Month budget	Actual	Variance	Year to date budget	Actual	Variance	Corres. period last year
Product A	300	294	(6)	1 800	1 294	(506)	300
Product B	110	117	7	650	833	183	88
Product C	440	320	(120)	2 600	1 800	(800)	360
Product D	250	300	50	1 500	1 400	(100)	280
Total	1 100	1 031	(69)	6 550	5 327	(1 223)	1 028

Value	Month budget	Actual	Variance	Year to date budget	Actual	Variance	Corres. period last year
Product A	3 000	5 000	2 000	18 000	22 000	4 000	3 000
Product B	2 200	1 400	(800)	13 000	10 000	(3 000)	1 750
Product C	2 200	1 600	(600)	13 000	9 000	(4 000)	1 800
Product D	2 500	3 000	500	15 000	14 000	(1 000)	2 800
Total	9 900	11 000	1 100	59 000	55 000	(4 000)	9 350

Exhibit 10.1 William's Widgets: sales analysis

Exhibit 10.1 shows one way of monitoring sales by volume and
value both on a monthly and a cumulative basis. The 'corresponding
period previous year' figure enables you to see at a glance if you
are ahead of last year's sales figures for the current month.

If you look at product A, you will note that the actual sales have
exceeded the budgeted sales by £2 000, even though the number
of units sold has decreased marginally. This is because the sale price
has been increased. Look at product B where the reverse has
happened. The sales by volume have increased but the sales value
has dropped dramatically due to achieving less than the budgeted
price.

These changes can be illustrated graphically, as shown in Exhibit
10.2. The price variance is shown on the y (vertical) axis and the
volume variance on the x (horizontal) axis. The total income, in
each case, is the area contained by the graph, i.e. by multiplying
the two sides. The budgeted sales price of £20 with sales of 110
units would generate £2 200 for the month. The actual sales price
of £12 with sales of 117 units generates £1 404.

This potentially gives two problems. If your direct costs are

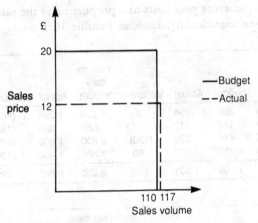

Exhibit 10.2 William's Widgets

constant, say at £8/unit, then the contribution per unit has dropped from £12 to £4. Although the sales volume has gone up slightly it has not increased sufficiently to cover the fixed costs attributed to this product, but the product is, at least, still making a positive contribution.

If you sell more than one product, the final variance may disguise substantial variances of the individual products. You must therefore look carefully at the individual product variances.

The presentation would be improved if the sales figures for the year were plotted as a graph with the forecast, actual and previous year's performance all shown together, as in Exhibit 10.3.

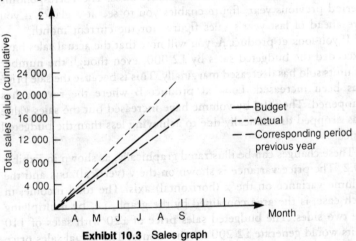

Exhibit 10.3 Sales graph

Sales figures are very important – you need to pick up trends quickly. A downturn in sales will require a cut-back in expenses if the trend continues for too long.

You should also look regularly at your order and enquiry position. Do you have enough orders for next month? Do you have enquiries that might quickly be turned into firm orders? If the answer to both of these is no, then you need to be working harder to promote your business.

Material and labour variances

As with sales variances, analysis of material and labour costs needs to look both at the cost and at the usage variance of raw materials or direct labour. One might be favourable, but the other might be unfavourable.

Gabriel runs a business which manufactures sealed, double glazed window units for the building trade. He has budgeted for the year to pay £20 per square metre for glass. The average size of window is 0.25 sq m which requires 0.5 sq m of glass. However, he budgets for wastage and breakage to add a further 0.25 sq m per window. Thus each window, on average, costs £15 for glass.

After one month, Gabriel compares his actual costs with his budget. The price of glass has risen to £22/sq m. However, his average usage is 0.6 sq m.

The variance can be calculated as follows:

Budget	0.75 sq m × £20	£15
Actual	0.6 sq m × £22	£13.20
Variance	(favourable)	£1.80

This can also be looked at graphically as shown in Exhibit 10.4. As with the sales variance, the price variance is shown on the y axis and the usage variance on the x axis. The total cost, in each case, is the area contained by the graph, i.e. by multiplying the two sides. sides.

Similar calculations can be employed for wage rates and labour efficiency.

It is important to understand why the figures are changing. It is quite possible for a favourable variance in raw material price to be cancelled by increased wastage, for example. This will not show

10

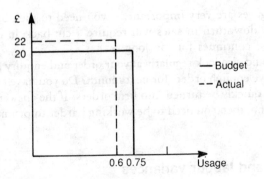

Exhibit 10.4 Gabriel's Glazing

up immediately in the analysis of the figures extracted from the accounting records, but needs to be monitored carefully.

Overheads variances

Variances in overheads are easier to monitor. For fixed overheads, any variance is simply caused by spending more or less money. Provided these costs are under control, and provided sales targets are being achieved, problems are unlikely to arise. If, however, margins are low and the targets are not being achieved then the sales revenue will not cover the fixed costs.

Variances of variable overheads are more difficult to track. Some should be watched carefully. If you have a high demand for electrical power, you will have a peak power meter installed and may find yourself on a tariff that changes if you use more power than agreed with your local electricity company. This should, therefore, be monitored in a similar way to raw material usage.

It has already been suggested that you monitor carefully the gross profit margin. In the same way, you should monitor specific overhead costs with the objective of restricting them to a percentage of the sales revenue. These figures can be compared year on year and against competitors if they are turned into ratios. For example:

$$\frac{\text{Selling costs}}{\text{Sales revenue}}$$

	Month budget	Actual	Variance	Year to date budget	Actual	Variance
Wages	2 000	2 000	0	12 000	11 500	500
Premises etc.	500	0	500	5 000	4 500	500
LP	350	450	(100)	7 000	6 800	200
Transport etc.	500	750	(250)	3 000	4 000	(1 000)
Advertising	1 000	1 500	(500)	6 000	4 000	2 000
Other	500	100	400	4 000	1 000	3 000
Total	4 850	4 800	50	37 000	31 800	5 200

Exhibit 10.5 Overheads analysis

Selling costs include all marketing and advertising costs as well as any sales people that you employ. Are the selling costs being contained? Is the effort put into selling reflected in the sales? Watching this figure carefully will also provide data to help in the preparation of demand curves.

$$\frac{\text{Administration costs}}{\text{Sales revenue}}$$

Are the administration costs being maintained? If they are very low, is customer service suffering?

$$\frac{\text{Distribution costs}}{\text{Sales revenue}}$$

Is your method of distribution the most efficient and effective? Is there scope to reduce distribution costs?

It is very difficult to control overheads. Left unchallenged, they will grow and eat into profits. Use ratios such as these to watch for sudden increases or variances. But also continually look to see if there are ways to reduce the total overhead burden.

The operating statement

Combining the sales income, direct costs and overhead costs enables you to prepare a monthly operating statement.

Each month you should compare your actual performance with your forecast both for the month and, ideally, for the year to date (see Exhibit 10.6).

	Month budget	%	Actual	%	Variance	Year to date budget	%	Actual	%	Variance
Sales revenue	9 900	100%	11 000	100%	(1 100)	59 000	100%	55 000	100%	4 000
less Direct costs:										
Materials	3 800	38%	4 650	42%	(850)	20 800	35%	23 000	42%	(2 200)
Sub-contract		0%		0%	0		0%		0%	0
Other		0%		0%	0		0%		0%	0
Total direct	3 800	38%	4 650	42%	(850)	20 800	35%	23 000	42%	(2 200)
Gross profit	6 100	62%	6 350	58%	(250)	38 200	65%	32 000	58%	6 200
less Overheads:										
Wages	2 000	20%	2 000	18%	0	12 000	20%	11 500	21%	500
Premises etc.	500	5%	0	0%	500	5 000	8%	4 500	8%	500
HLP	350	4%	450	4%	(100)	7 000	12%	6 800	12%	200
Transport etc.	500	5%	750	7%	(250)	3 000	5%	4 000	7%	(1 000)
Advertising	1 000	10%	1 500	14%	(500)	6 000	10%	4 000	7%	2 000
Other	500	5%	100	1%	400	4 000	7%	1 000	2%	3 000
Total overheads	4 850	49%	4 800	44%	50	37 000	63%	31 800	58%	5 200
Net operating profit	1 250	13%	1 550	14%	(300)	1 200	2%	200	0%	1 000

Exhibit 10.6 Operating statement

Monthly figures can, of course, be distorted by exceptional items, like a big order or a series of quarterly costs all falling due at the same time. However, these should have been allowed for in the forecast, so should not come as a surprise.

Don't forget that you may not be able to spend the profit! In times of heavy capital expenditure it is possible to be operating profitably when the cashflow is strongly negative. Similarly, you may have working capital tied up in stock or you may still be owed a lot by your customers.

This is the kind of report which should be generated easily if you have a computerised accounting system. You will have to stipulate which costs codes are direct and which are overhead costs. This will enable you, however, to allocate costs by product and to determine which products or services are most profitable.

Particularly note the gross profit margin. You will quickly discover the profit margin required to cover all your fixed costs. Newsagents, for example, work on a margin of 16 – 22 per cent; fashion shops might expect 40 – 50 per cent; manufacturers might aim for 60 – 80 per cent depending on the product. If it is falling, it could be a sign of trouble. Has wastage increased? Has the cost increased? Service business with no, or very low, direct costs, whilst they will have a very high margin, may not find it a helpful figure to watch.

The cash flow statement

10

The operating statement is like a profit and loss account, though it generally omits items such as depreciation which do not involve a movement of cash. It shows you the net trading profit that your business is achieving. It does not, however, give any indication of how liquid you are. It is therefore worthwhile to prepare a monthly cashflow statement as shown in Exhibit 10.7, or you can use the 'actual' column on your annual cashflow forecast if you use one with forecast and actual columns for each month. The cashflow statement reflects when money is received or expended and includes items such as drawings, VAT or tax, which are not regarded as trading expenses. The cashflow statement is the easiest to produce, because all the figures should be readily available from your cash book.

Managing the net cashflow can be more important in the short term than managing the net profit, because it allows for the timing of receipts and payments as well as for the amounts.

	Month budget	Actual	Variance	Year to date budget	Actual	Variance
Cash receipts						
Sales – cash			0			0
– credit	9 900	3 800	(6 100)	59 000	47 800	(11 200)
VAT	1 485	570	(915)	8 850	7 170	(1 680)
Sales of assets			0			0
Other receipts			0			0
Total	11 385	4 370	(7 015)	67 850	54 970	(12 880)
Cash payments						
Purchases – cash			0			0
– credit	3 800	3 150	650	20 800	21 500	(700)
Wages	2 000	2 000	0	12 000	11 500	500
Overheads	2 850	2 800	50	25 000	20 300	4 700
Capital	2 000	2 000	0	5 000	2 000	3 000
VAT	1 298	1 193	105	7 620	6 570	1 050
Loan repayments	500	500	0	3 000	3 000	0
Drawings	1 000	1 000	0	6 000	6 000	0
Other			0			0
Total	13 448	12 643	805	79 420	70 870	8 550
Net cashflow	(2 063)	(8 273)	(6 210)	(11 570)	(15 900)	(4 330)
Balance at start						
Cash	3 492	5 373		13 000	13 000	
Overdraft						
Balance at end						
Cash		1 430			1 430	
Overdraft		(2 900)			(2 900)	

Exhibit 10.7 Cashflow statement

Aged debtors

Some form of aged debtors report will be produced by most computer systems. Usually the debt will be listed for each customer. This is one of the most useful reports available, and is often the prime reason for installing a computerised accounting system.

Even if you do not have a computer, you should easily be able to derive a list of aged debtors from your sales ledger.

Calculate the average debt collection period. Has it got better – or worse? Are your customers paying promptly? Clearly, a reduction in the collection period will improve your cashflow.

	Current month	30 days	60 days	90 days	over 90 days	Total
This month	8 000	4 800	1 200	100	0	14 100
Last month	9 000	3 400	900			13 300

Top ten debtors

Debtors	Current month	30 days	60 days	90 days	over 90 days	Total	Credit limit
J Bloggs		2 800				2 800	3 000
D Smith	500		200	100		800	1 000
Crumbs Ltd	5 000	2 000				7 000	10 000
Ballyhoo	2 500		1 000			3 500	5 000
						0	
						0	
Total	8 000	4 800	1 200	100	0	14 100	

Debtors' turnover ratio, $d = \dfrac{\text{Sales}}{\text{Average debtors}} = \dfrac{55\ 000}{13\ 700} = 4$

Average collection period $= 365/d = 91$ days

Exhibit 10.8   Aged debtors

Aged creditors

Normally people are more concerned with getting their money in than paying out on time! However, payment outside of the terms of credit can lead to bad feeling and disruption of supplies. This report can serve as a check on the work of the accounts payable department to ensure that payments are being made within a reasonable period. An extension in the credit period taken will obviously improve your cashflow, but you need to beware of upsetting your suppliers.

Stock

You should watch the total amount of stock that you are carrying and aim to keep it as low as possible, commensurate with keeping sufficient raw materials to keep production going and sufficient finished goods to satisfy your customers.

It is very easy to tie up too much working capital in maintaining high stock levels, so monitor your stock carefully. As with sales and

10

	Current month	30 days	60 days	90 days	over 90 days	Total
This month	5 000	7 000	500	0	0	12 500
Last month	4 000	3 000	2 000			9 000

Top ten creditors

Creditors	Current month	30 days	60 days	90 days	over 90 days	Total	Credit limit
Richard Harvey	1 000	1 500				2 500	3 000
Tinker & Wood Ltd		500	500			2 000	1 000
Vehicle Supplies Ltd		2 000				2 000	10 000
Matsupplies	4 000	3 000				7 000	5 000
						0	
						0	
Total	5 000	7 000	500	0	0	12 500	

Creditors' turnover ratio, $c = \dfrac{\text{Sales}}{\text{Average debtors}} = \dfrac{55\,000}{10\,750} = 5$

Average collection period $= 365/c = 71$ days

Exhibit 10.9 Aged creditors

direct costs, stock should be monitored on an individual product basis.

It is normal to calculate the stock turnover ratio, or else to calculate the average period before goods are sold. In the example, the ratio is 14 times per year. Note that the turnover period has used 365 days. If, as suggested in Chapter 4, you use working days the calculation becomes $252/14 = 18$ working days. Do you know what the turnover ratio should be for your business? In the bookshop trade, for example, it should be about 4. That is, the stock is sold four times over during the year. This suggests, as you would expect, that bookshops have to carry a lot of stock and have, therefore, considerable working capital tied up. Other businesses turn over stock considerably faster and consequently tie up less working capital.

Most service sector businesses, other than retailing, have limited stock requirements and probably do not need to worry about their stock control too much.

Product A

	Month budget	Actual	Year to date budget	Actual
Start of period	1 500	1 500	1 500	1 500
Purchases	1 200	2 400	7 200	9 300
Stock used	1 200	2 000	7 200	8 800
End of period	1 500	1 900	1 500	2 000
Average	1 500	1 700	1 500	1 750

$$\text{Stock turnover ratio} = \frac{\text{Cost of sales}}{\text{Average stock}} = \frac{2\,000 \times 12}{1\,700} = \frac{24\,000}{1\,700} = 14.12 \text{ times p.a.}$$

Stock turnover period = 26 days

All products

	Month budget	Actual	Year to date budget	Actual
Start of period	2 500	4 000	3 000	2 000
Purchases	3 200	4 000	18 000	22 350
Stock used	3 800	4 650	20 800	23 000
End of period	1 900	3 350	200	1 350
Average	2 200	3 675	1 600	1 675

Exhibit 10.10 Stock control

The balance sheet

10

Once all the figures are available for all the analysis described above, you are also in a position to prepare the balance sheet.

Some items may fluctuate considerably from month to month. Others, for example the fixed assets, will show little change. If changes in stock and work in progress are slow, it may be preferable to check the actual levels less frequently, say, quarterly or annually. You should, however, be able to calculate a value for stock and work in progress.

Unless you have computerised your book-keeping, you may decide to prepare this report less frequently than monthly. In that case, you must prepare an alternative monthly report which at least shows the cash available, the total debtors and the total creditors. These three figures enable you to calculate the quick ratio.

Comparing the current ratio (1.3) in Exhibit 10.11 with the target (at least 1.5) suggests that the business is somewhat exposed. As

	Last month	Current month	Change %
Fixed assets			
Land & buildings			
Plant & machines	5 000	5 000	0%
Fixtures etc.	3 500	3 500	0%
Motor vehicles	2 000	4 000	100%
Total fixed assets	10 500	12 500	19%
Current assets			
Stock, S	1 900	3 350	76%
Work in progress, S	1 800	1 229	− 32%
Finished goods, S	1 500	6 700	347%
Debtors	13 300	14 100	6%
Bank			
Cash	1 430		
Total current assets, A	19 930	25 379	27%
Current liabilities			
Creditors	9 000	12 500	39%
Overdraft		2 900	
Loans	4 500	4 000	− 11%
Tax			
Total current liabilities, L	13 500	19 400	44%
Net current assets	6 430	5 980	− 7%
Total net assets	16 930	18 480	9%
Represented by:			
Owners' capital	8 000	8 000	0%
Reserves	8 930	10 480	17%
Total capital employed	16 930	18 480	9%

$$\text{Current ratio} = A/L = \frac{25\ 379}{19\ 400} = 1.31$$

$$\text{Quick ratio} = (A - S)/L = \frac{14\ 100}{19\ 400} = 0.73$$

Exhibit 10.11 Balance sheet

explained in Chapter 4, quick assets are those in cash or easily turned into cash. To determine quick assets, deduct all stock (raw materials, work in progress and finished goods) from the current assets. Dividing by the liabilities gives the quick ratio. At 0.7, this is just about on the bottom limit of acceptability. However, if the element of the bank loan repayable in more than one year is omitted, the current ratio improves to 1.4. If all the bank loan is omitted, since the repayment terms are fixed, the current ratio improves further to 1.65 and the quick ratio to 0.9.

Contribution by product line

This report shows an alternative layout to Exhibit 10.6 (the operating statement). Many people prefer the former format with or without the overhead analysis.

Contribution is a more meaningful parameter than gross profit since all deductions are variable costs. In practice defining variable costs is a good deal more difficult than it first appears. The effort of splitting variable costs by product line for labour, material and 'other' will probably involve too much administration for a small firm.

The figures for William's Widgets are shown in Exhibit 10.12. Since his only variable costs are material costs it is very easy to calculate the contribution, which you should note is the same as the gross profit figure in the operating statement.

Look now at Exhibit 10.13 which shows an analysis of the two services offered by Gabriel's Glazing. They buy in materials whether for assembly and installation, or for installation only. They use sub-contract labour for the installation. Both of these figures are easy to derive. They have other variable costs, however, which are less easy to calculate but include travel to the site, power consumption, etc.

Which service is the most profitable? Why do you think Gabriel offers both services when it appears that installation only gives a better margin?

10

Capital expenditure report

This report will prove most useful if there is an ongoing programme of building works. Capital projects are almost invariably late and overspent. A report such as this, prepared quarterly, at least alerts management on a regular basis to potential problems.

	Budget (year to date)					Actual (year to date)				
	Sales revenue	Variable materials	Variable labour	Variable other	Contribution	Sales revenue	Variable materials	Variable labour	Variable other	Contribution
Assembly & installation	200 000	80 000	40 000	6 000	74 000	220 000	90 000	35 000	5 000	90 000
Installation only	100 000	10 000	20 000	3 000	67 000	50 000	5 000	10 000	3 500	31 500
	300 000	90 000	60 000	9 000	141 000	270 000	95 000	45 000	8 500	121 500

Exhibit 10.13 Gabriel's Glazing: contribution by product line

	Budget (year to date)					Actual (year to date)				
	Sales revenue	Variable materials	Variable labour	Variable other	Contribution	Sales revenue	Variable materials	Variable labour	Variable other	Contribution
Product A	18 000	7 200			10 800	22 000	8 800			13 200
Product B	13 000	4 300			8 700	10 000	4 250			5 750
Product C	13 000	4 300			8 700	9 000	3 950			5 050
Product D	15 000	5 000			10 000	14 000	6 000			8 000
	59 000	20 800	0	0	38 200	55 000	23 000	0	0	32 000

Exhibit 10.12 William's Widgets: contribution by product line

Project	Expected completion date	Estimate	Revised estimate	Expenditure to date
Vehicle	September	3 000	2 000	2 000
Total		3 000	2 000	2 000

Exhibit 10.14 Capital expenditure

For most small businesses this will probably be unnecessary, though do not forget to include all capital expenditure in your cashflow.

Labour turnover report

This report will primarily apply in businesses where large numbers of staff are employed. A high labour turnover figure can be significant because:

1. It may indicate dissatisfaction with working conditions or management.
2. High labour turnover can be expensive in retraining staff.

	Month of September At start	Starters	Leavers	At end
Manufacturing	15	2	3	14
Sales	2			2
Administration	2			2
Directors	3			3
	22	2	3	21

Exhibit 10.15 Labour turnover report

Management information systems

You have probably read or heard about management information systems. There is nothing mysterious or complicated about management information systems. They are simply procedures set up by managers, to ensure that data about the business is collected, recorded, reported and evaluated quickly and efficiently. That information is then used to check the progress of the business and to control it effectively.

We have covered a wide range of figures and ratios that it is possible to monitor – and there are many others. The key to an effective management information system is to ensure that you only monitor a small number of figures and that those figures are related back to the strategic objectives and the overall targets that you have set for your business.

If other people need to see the figures then ensure they get them quickly. If your system of financial control is to be successful, you need to have the figures quickly after the end of each month.

This book is concerned about financial systems and financial control, but your management information system should be set up to give you regular feedback on progress made towards all your strategic objectives. You should also aim to monitor external factors which may affect your business. Some are obvious, like interest rates.

Business	
Checked by	Date

SALES

Last year's gross sales

Previous year's gross sales

PROFITABILITY

Last year's profits

Previous year's profits

Profit margin on sales (Profit before interest & tax/sales)

LIQUIDITY

Current ratio (Current assets/Current liability)　(1.5–2.0)

Liquidity ratio (Liquid assets/Current liability)　(0.7–1.0)

SOLVENCY

Interest cover (Profit before interest & tax/interest)　(2.0–4.0)

Gearing

EFFICIENCY

Debtors' turnover ratio/average collection period

Creditors' turnover ratio/average payment period

Exhibit 10.16　Financial review

Review the figures with your staff

It was stated earlier that the relevant staff should be involved in drawing up the budget for your business. They should get copies of the figures as soon as they are available. In addition, however, you should have regular financial review meetings.

You may find it useful to summarise the figures in the format suggested in Exhibits 10.16 and 10.17. These are used by one local enterprise agency as crib-sheets when appraising prospective borrowers and when monitoring borrowers.

Business	Ref No
Checked by	Date
Are financial records complete to last month end? (If no, date to which records are complete) Are VAT and PAYE records maintained?	
State bank current account balance + deposit balances	+
State the overdraft facility	
Are VAT payments and PAYE payments current?	
Sales	
Are sales profitable?	
Are costs still the same?	
Firm orders + likely orders	+
Repeat orders	
Stock value/representing number of week sales	
WIP value/representing number of weeks sales	
Has business the capacity to meet deadlines?	
Can quality levels be maintained/reached?	
Date of next rent review?	
Are premises suitable?	
Planned capital expenditure	
Level of drawings	
Number of employees	F/T P/T
Any wage increases?	
Possible problems	
Further action?	

10

Exhibit 10.17 Monthly monitoring

It is all very well analysing variances and identifying problems. If you have staff with financial responsibilities you should ensure that you meet regularly to review the variances together; to decide what action, if any, needs to be taken; and, crucially, to decide who should be taking that action.

It is equally important, if everything is on target, to praise staff for achieving the plan. It is a frequent complaint that managers are quick to criticise but never give praise, so seize the opportunities when they present themselves.

Analysis of variances: conclusion and checklist

If you are going to monitor and control your business effectively you must:

- Prepare a budget which is realistic and achievable, though probably at least a little challenging also; and
- Ensure that you monitor performance regularly, at least monthly, against that budget.

You may feel that this is time-consuming and unnecessary, but it is absolutely essential if you are to remain in complete control of your business.

The important areas to watch are:

- Sales variances:
  — sales price variances;
  — sales volume variances.

- Material variances:
  — material cost variances;
  — material usage variances.

- Labour variances:
  — activity variances;
  — wages variances.

- Overheads variances.

- Operating statement.

- Cashflow statement.

- Aged debtors.

- Aged creditors.
- Stock.
- Balance sheet.

Are all your products making a positive contribution? Do all the contributions cover your fixed costs? Are you on target? Is the money coming in or are the aged debtors getting too large? Are you still profitable? Are you still liquid? Are you still solvent?

You may find that you do not need to monitor all of these figures – but you should quickly find out which ones are the crucial ones for your business.

Exercise

You are reviewing the monthly sales figures for the painting and decorating business referred to at the end of Chapter 6. Your original estimate of total sales for the month was 20 jobs at an average price (excluding VAT) of £520. This comprises £469 contribution towards labour and overhead costs and £51 for paint. Your actual sales were £11 000.

1. Is this sales figure good or bad?
2. What variances do you need to look at more closely?
3. One job missed the deadline so you had to pay overtime of £750 to complete it over a weekend. You consumed more paint than you expected during the month, costing you a further £200. What do you think about the figures now?

10

11 Using the figures

Introduction

Some of the figures derived from the previous two chapters will suggest the need for specific action. This chapter looks at a number of ways in which the figures should be used to ensure close control.

The previous chapter highlighted a number of areas where variances are likely to occur and suggested ways of discovering the real cause of the variances. For example, a variance in direct costs could be caused by a price rise or increased wastage. As a result, it should be obvious what action needs to be taken. This chapter will not, therefore, look at using all the figures derived in the last chapter. It will concentrate instead on a few tips which may be helpful.

Orders

Review your order book regularly. Do you have enough orders of sufficient size for your next trading period? If not, you need to market your business to win some extra business. If that is unsuccessful, are there ways in which you can cut the costs incurred by the business until orders pick up again?

Debtors

If your business is sending out sales invoices (i.e. selling on credit), then a tight grip must be kept to ensure the position is both known and acceptable.

Your sales ledger clearly shows all your outstanding sales invoices. Review them regularly, preferably on a weekly basis but at the very least on a monthly basis. If any customer is slow in paying you, chase them hard. There is no hard and fast rule about the length of credit that you can give customers, but 30 days is normal in many business sectors. In some it is considerably longer.

Issue all sales invoices as soon as possible after the work is done; the sooner it is issued the sooner, in general, it will be paid and your business will receive the money. This can then be used to pay for more goods or reduce your overdraft, thus saving bank interest.

If you are not paid within your agreed collection period, issue a statement. Some businesses get into the habit of never paying until a statement arrives. If you do not regularly send out statements, mark on your original invoice that statements will not be issued.

If you need the money urgently ring your customer and politely but firmly enquire when you will receive what is owed to you. Ring more than once if necessary. Be careful about being fobbed off with excuses, for example:

> 'The director is away and we can't get the cheque signed'
> 'It's in the post'

Note these and if it doesn't come within two days, ring again.

If, after several weeks the money is not forthcoming, and the debt is large enough, legal action may be necessary. This is the last resort so keep pursuing the customer with phone calls first. Legal action is expensive and takes up your valuable time, though smaller claims can be dealt with relatively quickly through the Small Claims in the County Court procedure. One trick adopted by some small business people, when owed money by large customers, is simply to sit in their reception area and wait until the cheque is produced.

As was explained earlier in Chapter 7 under the head 'Funding working capital', you may wish to look at factoring or invoice discounting to speed up the receipt of the money you are owed.

Credit references

If large orders from unknown customers are placed with you, it may make sense to obtain a credit reference. Ask for trade references and also for a bank reference. Consult a credit reference agency – Dun and Bradsheet is the most well known, but there may be a smaller one locally. For example, the North Eastern Trades Association is a non-profit organisation which provides credi references and will also chase bad debts. In addition, you may choose not to give too much credit until your customers have built up a good record of paying you promptly.

Creditors

Keeping control of the money you owe others can be done in a similar fashion to the way you control money owed to you. Review all the bills you have to pay at least monthly.

As mentioned earlier, many businesses do not record bills (i.e. purchase invoices) as they arrive. However, once they have been paid, they are properly filed and recorded in the cash book. This is not very satisfactory since you have little idea of the amount outstanding. Use a purchase ledger as described earlier. Mark when each bill is paid. Look to see if you get a discount for speedy payment. Do not upset your suppliers by delaying payment for too long, otherwise they may withdraw your credit facilities. It takes time to build up a good track record with suppliers, but when you do, working on credit becomes easier. To gain the most benefit, you need to take the maximum amount of credit possible without upsetting your suppliers, or destroying a good track record.

Economic order quantities

We discussed stock control earlier in relation to keeping track of stock and its usage. Do you wait until you have run out of raw materials before you re-order? Do you know the optimum amount to order at one time?

Simple stock control systems are usually designed so that when stock falls to a predetermined level, then you re-order. That level should provide sufficient stock to cover the expected delay between placing the order and receiving the goods, plus allow for a contingency.

11

Ian runs a business offering direct mail facilities to other businesses. As a result, he has to hold large stocks of envelopes. He knows from experience how many boxes of each size of envelope to hold as a minimum stock requirement.

He stacks his boxes in columns. On top of the minimum stock holding for each size, Ian places a red card. Further boxes are then stacked on top.

When the envelopes are used down to the red card, Ian knows that it is time to re-order.

Exhibit 11.1

Exhibit 11.1 gives one example of a very simple stock ordering reminder system. This can act as a back up to your stock record book. Most computerised book-keeping systems can include a stock control module if desired.

As explained earlier, you do not want to tie up too much working capital in stock. Costs of holding stock include rent on the space occupied, insurance, interest foregone on the money, etc. On the other hand, running out of raw materials can be extremely embarrassing. You may have to pay extra for rapid delivery of new stock. Production will be halted and you will lose sales. The process of ordering needs time and therefore costs money also. These costs can be shown graphically (see Exhibit 11.2). Adding the costs together gives a total cost curve. As can be seen there is an optimum order volume, Q at the trough in the curve.

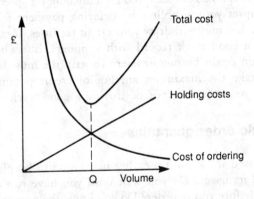

Exhibit 11.2

The economic order quantity, Q is given by the equation:

$$Q = \sqrt{\frac{2UO}{H}}$$

where U is the usage during a defined period, O is the cost of ordering and handling and H is the holding cost. Hopefully, this will provide you with a starting point to assess your ideal order quantities.

What is just-in-time stock control?

'Just-in-time' stock control has been around for a long time though it is primarily the Japanese who have developed it. The objective is that deliveries of raw materials or bought-in components should arrive just in time to be included in the process. This saves holding large amounts of stock tying up working capital and space. It is often difficult to organise without the muscle that Nissan or Toyota commands. It requires extremely good planning and can easily cause problems if delivery is 'just too late'.

However, do not think you have to be large to use a just-in-time delivery system. One businessman known to the author manufactures headboards for beds. He sells on customer service guaranteeing delivery within the week for orders placed at the beginning of the week. Because his premises are not very large, and because he cannot afford to tie up working capital in large stock holdings, he orders wood and upholstery every Thursday for delivery on the following Monday. Foam presents a fire risk so he is limited in the total amount he can store on his premises. As a result, he has foam delivered three times per week.

Once you get into the habit, just-in-time stock control (or nearly so in the example) is just as easy as any other system. A major advantage of just-in-time stock control is that the need to value raw material stock and finished goods stock is reduced substantially since stock no longer requires large amounts of working capital.

Shrinkage

Many businesses suffer from shrinkage (theft) and shop-lifting. Ideally your stock control system will indicate at an early stage if this is happening. You may need to take regular stock-checks. Does the amount of actual stock reconcile with your stock control book?

It is often difficult to prevent this completely. Take some simple precautions. Keep stock locked away. Ensure stock is deducted correctly in the control book and signed for. Be very vigilant.

Equipment leasing

If you decide to lease equipment, make sure that you read all the small print. Whilst the selling is carried out by your supplier, the leasing is done by a finance company. Often the conditions are more favourable for them than for you.

On the other hand, the lessor also has a responsibility to ensure the equipment keeps working even if the supplier can no longer support you!

Cash management

Do you have large sums of money simply sitting in a current account? Is it likely to be there for long? If you are lucky enough to have substantial cash balances, make it work for you. All the banks have special arrangements for putting large sums on deposit – frequently directly on the sterling money market. Interest rates are often within a couple of percentage points of the bank base rate. In general, the longer the period for which you are prepared to tie up your money, the better the rate of interest that can be obtained.

If your business is incorporated as a company, the banks will pay your interest gross. You will have to pay tax on it eventually, but in the mean time you have that extra money available either to invest and attract still further interest, or to use as working capital. You should note, however, that interest is taxed under a different schedule and this income cannot be offset against any trading losses or capital allowances.

If you think interest rates are likely to fall, you might consider buying government loan stock (known as gilt edged stocks). These can be bought and sold like shares, or for some stocks, through the Post Office. If you buy stock with a high interest rate, which is fixed until the stock matures, you will find that the capital value of the stock increases as interest rates fall. The reverse also occurs, however, so there is some risk attached, though the risk is limited.

Clearly, it makes sense not to become too illiquid by tying up all your spare cash for too long. If you are likely to need some or all of your cash quickly, do not put it into long-term investments.

You could also, of course, look at whether you should be investing some or all of your cash back into the business. Should you be upgrading equipment? Are there opportunities for expansion? Are there new business opportunities? Remember the tips in the chapter on capital appraisal, however. How do you get the best return on that money right now? Once again, it might be prudent not to use all of it in this way but to keep at least some for expanded working capital requirements.

Improving staff efficiency

Efficiency is usually a measure of a volume of activity. Do you believe that your staff are working as efficiently and effectively as possible? Are there ways in which you can improve that efficiency?

One way is to encourage more competition between staff, perhaps with performance bonuses and prizes. There is always the danger, however, of sabotage! What you require is to encourage the development of a team spirit, so that everyone pulls together for the good of the business. Perhaps a performance bonus based on total results might be appropriate. In this case, however, watch out for those not pulling their weight. Whilst they might be carried to start with, they will quickly cause resentment.

Would different machines improve efficiency? Do you regularly ask your staff for their suggestions? Do they see their work merely as 'a job' or something they want to do? Take an interest in career development. Encourage further training, even if it is not directly related to their work. Undertake regular appraisals. Praise staff when they do well. This is at least as important, and maybe more so, than criticising poor performance.

Lastly, keep all your staff well informed about the business's objectives, its performance and its progress. Do not spend all your time sitting behind a desk in an office with the door closed! Talk regularly to all your staff. Let them see that you are committed and they will try harder also. When the director of a business in the north-east built a new factory, he designed internal walls to be mostly glass. From his office he can see to all corners – and all the staff can see him as well. This all helps to build morale and maintain a happy workforce.

11

Improving capital efficiency

The only way to improve capital efficiency is to make it work harder for you. This is a lot more difficult than it sounds. One way is to employ less capital in the business, and to use more borrowed money. This increases the gearing and is unlikely to be popular with your bankers or other lenders.

Consider this example:

	Business A	Business B
Profit before interest and tax	20 000	20 000
less: interest	1 500	6 000
Net profit	18 500	14 000
Share capital	50 000	20 000
loans (at 15%)	10 000	40 000
	£60 000	£60 000
Gearing	17%	67%
Return on share capital (after interest)	37%	70%

Whilst the amount paid in interest is considerably higher, the return on shareholder's capital is also considerably higher. The banks, however, will prefer business A's gearing!

Using the figures: conclusion and checklist

Deriving the performance figures for a business is relatively straightforward. It is essential to understand what the figures are saying and to use those figures for effective control. In particular

- Constantly review your order position and look at ways of improving the marketing of your business.
- Chase your debtors for speedy payment.
- Review your creditors regularly and do not delay payment beyond your agreed terms.
- Review your raw material ordering procedures and aim for just in-time stock control.
- If you have any spare cash available, make it work for you in either short- or long-term investments – depending on your likely cash needs.

12 Using computers

ntroduction

is possible to use computers either to assist or to take over
ompletely all the data recording and calculation of the appropriate
gures and ratios for your management information system. There
re, of course, dangers in using computers. It is very easy to treat
ne output as gospel – remember that it is only as good as the
nformation that is entered. It is extremely helpful, therefore, to have
n understanding of the requirements of financial control. This makes
 more likely that errors will be spotted if they do occur and also
nat you will understand what the outputs mean.

ccounts on computer

here are a wide range of computerised accounting packages
vailable, which will provide everything from simple book-keeping
o sophisticated and comprehensive accounting packages providing
orecasting facilities, variance analysis, etc. It makes considerable
·nse, however, to start by keeping your books on a manual basis.
his enables you to understand the principles of book-keeping and
 discover for yourself how to derive the figures that you want on
 regular basis. As stated earlier, it will also help you to spot any
rors once you do computerise.

The first financial system that people usually computerise is that
° payroll. Since the calculations are routine and tedious, payroll
nds itself extremely easily to being computerised, with the further
dvantage that you can immediately print payslips, autopay lists,
onthly and year-to-date summaries, etc.

If you decide to computerise all your accounts, think carefully
>out the functions that you require. Compare the functions available
 a number of different packages. If you are registered for VAT
>u are supposed to seek the agreement of the VAT office before

Code	Description	This month	This month %	This year	This year %	Last year	Budget
100	SALES						
110	MAILING						
111	Handling fees	191.20	5%	7 924.10	20%		25%
119	MAILING TOTAL	191.20	5%	7 924.10	20%		25%
120	POSTAGE						
121	Postage	1 215.14	33%	14 701.22	37%		29%
122	Courier	32.20	1%	62.20	0%		0%
120	POSTAGE TOTAL	1 247.34	33%	14 763.42	37%		29%
140	DESIGN/DPT/WP						
141	Design/Artwork		0%		0%		0%
142	DTP	813.54	22%	2 586.54	7%		3%
143	Word process	13.05	0%	13.05	0%		0%
149	DESIGN TOTAL	826.59	22%	2 599.59	7%		3%
197	Sales discount						
199	TOTAL SALES	3 738.66	100%	39 758.39	100%		100%
300	PURCHASES						
310	MAILING COSTS						
311	Franking supply		0%		0%		
319	MAIL COST TOTAL		0%		0%		
320	POSTAGE COSTS						
321	Postage	1 490.00	40%	14 190.00	36%		
322	Courier		0%		0%		
329	POST COST TOTAL	1 490.00	40%	14 190.00	36%		

Code	Item	This month	%	This year	%	
341	Freelance fees		0%		0%	
342	Linotype output		0%		0%	
343	Graphic goods	7.20	0%	36.29	0%	
349	DESIGN COST TOTAL	7.20	0%	36.29	0%	
399	TOTAL PURCHASES	2 531.76	68%	20 497.69	52%	40%
400	EXPENSES & OVERHEADS					
410	STAFF COST					
411	Wages	1 269.52	34%	11 023.45	28%	
412	NI/PAYE	987.53	26%	5 139.81	13%	
413	Expenses		0%	11.94	0%	
415	Misc wages	100.00	3%	300.00	1%	
416	Freelance	1 480.05	40%	1 960.05	5%	
419	WAGE COST TOTAL	3 837.10	103%	18 435.25	46%	
499	TOTAL EXPENSES	5 690.13	152%	31 761.39	80%	50%

TRADING (PROFIT/LOSS) SUMMARY

	This month		This year	
Sales:	3 738.66	100%	39 758.39	100%
− Purchases:	2 531.76	68%	20 497.69	52%
Gross profit:	1 206.90	32%	19 260.70	48%
+ Other income:	662.17	18%	7 541.63	19%
− Expenses:	5 690.13	152%	31 761.39	80%
Net profit:	−3 821.06	−102%	−4 959.06	−12%

Exhibit 12.1 Tyne Thames Technology Ltd trading (profit and loss)

12

you computerise your accounts. They will want to be assured that there is a proper audit trail built into the software.

Once you have bought the software, read the instructions extremely carefully. As is often the case with software, the installation and initial setting up routines are the hardest part.

You will need to code everything – all your sales and all your expenditure. Look back at your last few months records to see what could usefully be coded separately. Be as logical as possible. Whilst it is always possible to add extra codes later, you may lose the initial logical layout.

Entering the data

Rather than entering every sales or purchase invoice immediately it appears, I would suggest that you collect them altogether. They can then be entered as a batch every few days. However, you should not use this as an excuse not to enter the data regularly.

You will need to take care that entries are properly coded, that the data is entered only once and that they are entered into the correct ledger. Whilst safeguards and validation checks are usually built into the software, it is still possible to enter data incorrectly, which will then affect all the figures. If errors are made, then do refer to the documentation to ensure that the corrections are made properly. If, for example, a sales invoice is issued twice, then a credit note needs to be entered through the sales ledger rather than simply correcting the cash book.

You will probably find it helpful to consult with your accountant when computerising your accounts. They will almost certainly have experience of a range of software and will be able to advise on the most appropriate software for your business. Furthermore, they will probably be able to help you set it up in a way that is not only simple for you to use, but also helps them to do their job at the end of each year.

Exhibits 12.1 and 12.2 show an extract from a trading profit and loss account and a balance sheet for Tyne Thames Technology Ltd. In particular, note the coding system that has been used, which matches, as far as possible, sales and direct sales.

What problems does this business have? What would be your first steps to solve those problems?

Note that the figures shown are only an extract from the accounts so they do not give the totals shown! Note also that the opening position on the balance sheet has been omitted, so the figures do

Code	Description	This month	Balance	Opening balance
500	CAPITAL			
511	Retained profit	– 3 821.06	1 455.10	
528	Opening balance	0.00	11 153.24	
599	TOTAL CAPITAL	– 3 821.06	12 608.34	
600	LIABILITIES			
699	TOTAL LIABILITY			
700	FIXED ASSETS			
713	Fixtures	0.00	361.36	
714	Other equipment	0.00	49.43	
799	TOTAL FIXED ASSETS	0.00	410.79	
800	CURRENT ASSETS			
811	Sales control	1 672.81	5 865.29	
841	Bank current account	– 1 715.59	3 877.86	
842	Bank deposit account		10 000.00	
847	Petty cash	– 23.87	60.95	
899	TOTAL CURRENT ASSETS	– 66.65	19 804.10	
900	CURRRENT LIABILITIES			
911	Purchase control	3 401.82	5 393.02	
921	VAT control	352.59	429.19	
922	Wages/PAYE control	0.00	1 786.34	
999	TOTAL CURRENT LIABILITIES	3 754.41	7 606.55	

BALANCE SHEET SUMMARY

Capital employed		12 608.34
Fixed assets	410.79	
Current assets	19 804.10	
less: Current liabilities	7 606.55	
Working capital	12 197.55	
Total assets		12 608.34

Exhibit 12.2 Tyne Thames Technology Ltd: balance sheet

not give a fair representation of the business. You should, however, look at the ways the figures have been coded. These codes need to be used whenever data is entered to ensure the sales or costs are included in the correct place.

As you can see, the software is able automatically to produce monthly and year-to-date profit and loss accounts and a balance sheet at the end of each month.

Good financial software will enable you to input your cashflow forecast on a monthly basis, and also retain your last year's actual performance for comparison. Each month, after you have input the actual figures, the software will produce a variance analysis automatically. Remember, as explained earlier, that the variance figures may hide price and usage variance so these need to be looked at separately.

Use of spreadsheets

There is a wide range of spreadsheet packages available that can speed up the preparation of financial forecasts and give considerable help in the analysis of actual results giving speedy comparisons with budgets. Well-known packages include Lotus 1 – 2 – 3 and Quattro. All the exhibits in this book involving figures were prepared using Quattro Pro. In addition to calculating figures rapidly, a good spreadsheet will also enable you to produce graphs quickly and accurately.

A spreadsheet can be likened to a large sheet of paper, divided into 256 columns and 8 192 rows. An example of the opening screen of Quattro Pro is shown in Exhibit 12.3.

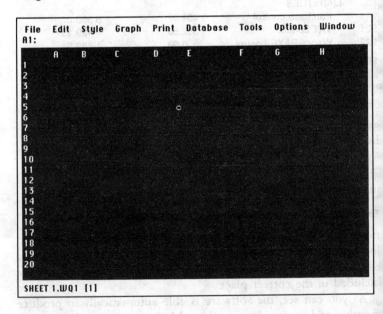

Exhibit 12.3 Quattro Pro: opening screen

The top line shows the menu of commands available. The next row shows the contents of the current cell. In this case, the cell is A1 and it is empty. The next row labels the columns. The column on the left-hand side of the screen numbers the rows. The bottom row is the name of the current file.

The cursor can be quickly and easily moved around the screen by use of the arrow keys. Figures, labels or formulae can then be entered. The use of formulae means that rows or columns can easily be totalled. Results can be transferred to other locations on the spreadsheet. A spreadsheet package is particularly useful, therefore, to prepare cashflow forecasts together with the associated profit and loss account and balance sheet. This is probably the most helpful function a computer can perform. Once the budgets have been set and the forecasts prepared, it is possible to look at effects of changes in sales or costs (i.e. perform a sensitivity analysis). If you don't think your budget is completely realistic, it is extremely easy to change a few of the figures. Remember, however, that hard work is still required to prepare the figures initially. Do not fall into the mistake of assuming they must be correct because the computer says so!

Many spreadsheet packages incorporate a wide range of statistical, mathematical and financial functions. Quattro Pro, for example, will calculate depreciation amounts totally automatically. One drawback, however, is that since many of the packages originate in the USA, the financial functions are not always absolutely suited for the UK.

Let us look at an example. You will recall that Exhibit 8.3 showed a calculation of net present value for Charlton's Chocolates. Look at it again in Exhibit 12.4.

On screen, the figures look exactly the same as in the earlier exhibit (except for the lines which have been omitted for clarity). However, the spreadsheet has performed all the calculations.

Look at cell C7, for example. The contents of cell C7 is $1/((1 + F4)^{\wedge}(A7))$. This may look quite complicated, but is actually quite simple.

You will recall from Chapter 8 that the discount factor is given by:

$$\frac{1}{(1 + r)^n}$$

where r is the rate and n is the number of years. The equation in cell C7, takes the rate, which is located in cell F4, adds it to 1, raises

File	Edit	Style	Graph	Print	Database	Tools	Options	Window

A1:

	A	B	C	D	E	F	G	H
1								
2								
3	Year		Cashflow	Discount		Present		Rate
4	0			Factor		Value		0.13
5	0		-25 000	1.00		-25 000		
6	1		6 000	0.88		5 310		
7	2		9 000	0.78		7 048		
8	3		12 000	0.69		8 317		
9	4		15 000	0.61		9 200		
10	NPV					4 874		
11								
12								
13								
14								
15								
16								
17								
18								
19								
20								

SHEET 1.WQ1 [1]

Exhibit 12.4

it to the power of the contents of cell A7 and then divides 1 b
the result.

Now look at cell D7. Its contents are $+B7*C7$. In order words
it is the result of multiplying the contents of the two cells B7 and C7

The total net present value is found by adding up the presen
values for each year, so the content of cell D10 is @sum(D5.D9)
Rather than using the $+$ sign, and noting every cell individually
spreadsheet packages include commands to sum rows and column
quickly.

Let us look at another example. Suppose you wish to calculat
the annual percentage rate (APR) knowing that you are being charge
2.2 per cent per month for your credit card.

In cell A1, you type the monthly interest rate as a decimal number
In cell B1, you type $((A1 + 1)\hat{\ }12) - 1$. This means, take the content
of cell A1, add 1, raise to the power of 12, and subtract one fror
the result.

For a monthly interest rate of 2.2 per cent (0.022) this gives a.
APR of 29.84 per cent (i.e. 0.2984). Some spreadsheets enable yo
to enter numbers as decimals, but will display them as percentage
thus saving multiplication or division by 100 at regular intervals

It will take time and careful preparation to set up a spreadshee
to give helpful and usable information. Once set up, however,

will speed up considerably the preparation of all the figures and ratios that you are ever likely to need.

If you use a spreadsheet to track monthly sales and costs, then it will probably be able to draw you a variety of graphs, including sales graphs, profit graphs, break-even graphs, etc. If you include the previous year's data, you will be able to produce an instant graphical comparison.

Most packages are so cheap these days that, if you have a computer, the best advice is to buy a spreadsheet and play with it.

Using computers: conclusion and checklist

Computers are extremely helpful in speeding up calculations, particularly where the same calculations are to be performed every month. The most useful functions for the small business will be:

- Accounts.
- Financial control through the use of spreadsheets or accounting packages.
  Budgeting and the preparation of financial forecasts.

12

Appendix 1   Glossary

Absorption costing   A method of costing that does not distinguish between fixed and variable costs in the calculation of total cost; the total costs are simply divided by the total number of units produced.

Contribution   The amount contributed by a sale is the income generated by that sale less the variable cost of producing that product.

Cost of sales   The costs which are clearly attributable to a product.

Debt   Money which has been borrowed to finance the business. Debt might be in the form of an overdraft, a term loan or a debenture.

Depreciation   The amount charged to the profit and loss account each year to represent the wear and tear of machinery, equipment or industrial buildings.

Direct cost   A cost which is directly attributable to a product or service, such as raw materials. The direct cost will be the same for each unit, but will clearly vary with the total number of units.

Drawings   If you are self-employed as a sole trader or partner you will draw money from the business at regular intervals. Known as drawings, this is an advance against profit. Remember that you are taxed on the profit, not on your drawings.

Efficiency ratios   These are a measure of the efficiency of the business, for example, in collecting debts, in paying creditors, in keeping stock to a minimum, etc.

Equity   The equity in a business is the (shareholders') capital introduced by the owners, together with any retained earnings.

Expenses   A general term which can mean all the costs of a business, but normally used to signify overhead expenses (as opposed to direct costs).

Fixed costs   Costs which, generally speaking, are fixed for the business for a reasonable length of time, and not dependent on the number of units produced. These include, for example, rent, rates, salaries, etc.

Gearing   A measure of debt as a proportion of total finance (i.e. debt plus equity).

Gross profit   Normally regarded as the sales income less the direct costs. For many small businesses this will be the same as the contribution.

Interest cover   A measure of the ease with which a business can meet its interest requirements. The interest cover is the net profit before interest and tax divided by the interest payable for the same period. Lenders tend to look at this figure!

Invariable costs   Costs which do not vary with the number of units produced.

Liquidity   A measure of the working capital or cash available to a business to enable it to meet its liabilities as they fall due. Liquidity ratios include the current ratio and the quick ratio (also known as the 'acid test').

Marginal costing   Marginal cost is the extra cost of producing one extra unit. Marginal costing compares the marginal revenue of selling the extra unit with the marginal cost.

Net profit   The actual profit made by the business after the deduction of all expenses. Remember that if you are self-employed, your drawings are not regarded as an expense. Tax is not regarded as an expense.

Net worth   Total assets less total liabilities. Equivalent term to 'net assets'. Equal to shareholders' capital.

Profitability   A series of measures which show how profitable a business is. These include gross profit and net profit. Probably the best measure is 'profit before interest and tax', i.e. the sales income less all the direct costs and all the overhead costs except interest. The profit margin is PBIT/sales.

Revenue   The income generated by the business for a specific period.

Solvency   A measure of a business's ability to pay its bills as they fall due. If it cannot, then it is insolvent.

Variable costs   Costs which vary with the level of production. These clearly include direct costs such as raw materials. However, other costs, such as power consumption, may also vary with the level of production. These need to be allocated in some way so that the price of the product relates to the labour and resources consumed in its production.

Variance   The difference between budgeted figures and actual figures. Remember that a variance may be a combination of a cost variance and a volume variance, so take care to understand the implications. If a variance is too high, then corrective action will have to be taken to bring the business back on course.

Appendix 2 Further reading

If you want to read in more detail about accounting in business, I would recommend:

Bull, R. J. *Accounting in Business*, Butterworths, 1980
Drucker, P. *The Practice of Management*, Pan, 1968
Nobes, C. *Pocket Accountant*, The Economist Publications, 1985

Appendix 3 Control forms for your own use

Form 1 Sales analysis

Volume	Month Budget	Actual variance	Year to date Budget	Actual variance	Corres. period last year
Product					
Product					
Product					
Product					
Product					
Product					
Product					
Total					

Value	Month Budget	Actual variance	Year to date Budget	Actual variance	Corres. period last year
Product					
Product					
Product					
Product					
Product					
Product					
Product					
Total					

Form 2   Overheads analysis

	Month Budget Actual variance	Year to date Budget Actual variance
Wages		
Premises etc.		
HLP		
Transport etc.		
Advertising		
Other		
Other		
Other		
Other		
Other		
Total		

Form 3   Operating statement

	Month Budget % Actual % Variance		Year to date Budget % Actual
Sales revenue			

less: Direct costs
  Material
  Sub-contract
  Other
Total direct			

Gross profit			

less: Overheads
  Wages
  Premises etc.
  HLP
  Transport etc.
  Advertising
  Other			

Total overheads			
Net operating profit			

Form 4   Cashflow statement

	Month		Year to date	
	Budget Actual variance		Budget Actual variance	
CASH RECEIPTS				
Sales – cash				
– credit				
VAT				
Sales of assets				
Other receipts				
Total				
CASH PAYMENTS				
Purchases – cash				
– credit				
Wages				
Overheads				
Capital				
VAT				
Loan repayments				
Drawings				
Other				
Total				
Net cash flow				
Balance at start				
Balance at end				
Cash				
Overdraft/Loan				

App 3

Form 5 Aged debtors

	Current month	30 days	60 days	90 days	over 90 days	Total	
This month							A
Last month							B

Top ten debtors

Debtors	Current month	30 days	60 days	90 days	over 90 days	Total	Cred limit
Total							

Debtors' turnover ratio, $d = \dfrac{\text{Sales}}{\text{Average debtors}} = \dfrac{\text{Sales this month}}{(A+B)/2}$

Average collection period = $365/d =$

Form 6 Aged creditors

	Current month	30 days	60 days	90 days	over 90 days	Total	
This month							A
Last month							B

Top ten creditors

Creditors	Current month	30 days	60 days	90 days	over 90 days	Total	Cred limit
Total							

Creditors' turnover ratio, $c = \dfrac{\text{Sales}}{\text{Average debtors}} = \dfrac{\text{Sales this month}}{(A+B)/2}$

Average collection period = $365/c =$

Form 7 Stock control (Product:)

	Month Budget	Actual	Year to date Budget	Actual
Start of period				
Purchases				
Stock used				
End of period				
Average				

Stock turnover ratio $= \dfrac{\text{Cost of sales}}{\text{Average stock}} = \dfrac{\text{Value of stock used}}{\text{Average stock level}}$

Stock turnover period =

Stock control – all products

	Month Budget	Actual	Year to date Budget	Actual
Start of period				
Purchases				
Stock used				
End of period				
Average				

Form 8   Balance sheet

	Last month	Current month	Change %
Fixed assets			
Land & buildings			
Plant & machines			
Fixtures etc.			
Motor vehicles			
Total fixed assets			
Current assets			
Raw material stock, S			
Work in progress, S			
Finished goods, S			
Debtors			
Bank			
Cash			
Total current assets, A			
Current liabilities			
Creditors			
Overdraft			
Loans			
Tax			
Total current liabilities, L			
Net current assets			
Total net assets			
Represented by:			
Owners' capital			
Reserves			
Total capital employed			

Current ratio $= A/L =$ _____

Quick ratio $= (A - S)/L =$ _____

Form 9 Contribution by product line

	Budget (year to date)					Actual (year to date)				
	Sales revenue	Variable materials	Variable labour	Variable other	Cont.	Sales revenue	Variable materials	Variable labour	Variable other	Cont.
Product										
Product										
Product										
Product										
Product										
Product										
Product										
Product										
Product										
Total										

App 3

Form 10   Labour turnover report

	Month of At start	Starters	Leavers	At end
Manufacturing				
Sales				
Administration				
Directors				
Total				

Form 11   Capital expenditure

Project	Expected completion date	Estimate	Revised estimate	Expenditure to date
Total				

Appendix 4 Answers to the exercises

Chapter 3

1. £7 877 187
2. £7 809 760
3. £18 912 691 – if you include 'loans'.
   £17 914 001 – if you exclude 'loans'. Although it is not apparent from the exhibit, the loans are repayable in more than one year.
4. No.
5. Given the high level of fixed assets and the ease with which Young's could borrow money, the answer is yes.
6. From the figures, it would appear not, though the detailed accounts do, in fact, show that most of the bank borrowing is term loan or bills of exchange. Only £2.8m is borrowed as overdraft. Only £1.9m of the creditors is trade creditors, so in fact Young's is reasonably liquid.

Chapter 4

1. 0.42 (or 0.44 if you use the revised figure for current liabilities given above).
2. Poorly.
3. 0.18.
4. 0.12 (i.e. 12 per cent).
5. Because of the high value of their properties. If the revaluation reserve is omitted, the gearing is still only 32 per cent.
6. 0.10 (i.e. 10 per cent).

Chapter 6

1. The total costs are:

	Five staff @ £10 000	£50 000
	Overheads	£25 000
	Drawings	£20 000

Your drawings are apparently net, so you need to allow for tax	£7 500
You should allow a profit margin for reinvestment, say	£10 000
Total costs	£112 500

If there are 240 jobs pa, then the price for an average job = 112 500/240 = 468.75

You will need to add VAT @ 15% 70.31

£539.06

Note that this does not include materials which will have to be added. If the materials are fairly standard, for example, paint, then you could include it as part of your total costs. If materials costs vary dramatically, then add it afterwards.

2. (a) 3 hours.
   (b) Efficiency ratio = standard hours/acutal hours = 3/2.5 = 120 per cent.
   (c) You need to make a number of assumptions here. If everyone has 20 days' holiday and all their statutory holiday, they expect to work 233 days of the year. Allowing an average, say, of 5 days' sick leave reduces this to 228 days. If everyone works 37.5 hours per week (i.e. 7.5 hours/day), the total hours available are $228 \times 7.5 \times 5 = 8\ 550$ hours pa, equivalent to an average of 164.4 hours per week. This is the number of standard hours on which you base your budget.
   (d) The capacity ratio = actual hours available/budgeted hours = 130/164.4 = 79 per cent.

Chapter 8

You need to calculate the net present value for each option. Use a discount rate of 14 per cent.

	Year	Cashflow	Discount Factor	Present Value
Lathe:	0	− 17 500	1.00	− 17,500
	1	9 000	0.88	7 895
	2	9 000	0.77	6 925
	3	9 000	0.67	6 075
	4	9 000	0.59	5 329
	Net Present Value			8 723
Mill:	0	− 18 000	1.00	− 18 000
	1	7 000	0.88	6 140
	2	7 000	0.77	5 386
	3	7 000	0.67	4 725
	4	7 000	0.59	4 145
	5	7 000	0.52	3 636
	6	7 000	0.46	3 189
	Net Present Value			9 221

Both options give a positive NPV so you will get a better return by investing in a new machine compared to leaving your money in the bank. The milling machine gives a slightly better return so you should choose that option.

App 4

Chapter 10

1. Expected sales are 20 jobs × £520 = £10 400. Actual sales have exceeded expected sales so this appears good on the face of it but you cannot really answer the question until you have looked more closely at how the figures are derived.
2. Labour variance and materials variance.
3. Let us look at the figures in some detail:

	Expected	Actual	Variance
Sales	10 400	11 000	600
Costs			
Materials	1 020	1 220	(200)
Staff	4 170	4 920	(700)
Other Overheads	4 375	4 375	
Profit	835	485	(350)

The sales were higher than expected by £600, but this is more than cancelled out by the increased costs of £950. Whilst this is not disastrous, it is worse than forecast.

Index